The Song of Songs

The
Song of Songs
Codes of Love

Edwin M. Good

With an afterword by
Anita Sullivan

 CASCADE *Books* • Eugene, Oregon

THE SONG OF SONGS
Codes of Love

Copyright © 2015 Edwin M. Good. All rights reserved. Except for brief quotations in critical publications or reviews, no part of this book may be reproduced in any manner without prior written permission from the publisher. Write: Permissions. Wipf and Stock Publishers, 199 W. 8th Ave., Suite 3, Eugene, OR 97401.

Cascade Books
An Imprint of Wipf and Stock Publishers
199 W. 8th Ave., Suite 3
Eugene, OR 97401

www.wipfandstock.com

ISBN 13: 978-1-62564-895-2

Cataloguing-in-Publication data:

Good, Edwin M. (Edwin Marshall), 1928–2014

    The Song of Songs : codes of love / Edwin M. Good ; with an Afterword by Anita Sullivan.

    x + 160 p. ; 22 cm. Includes bibliographical references.

    ISBN 13: 978-1-62564-895-2

    1. Bible. Song of Solomon—Commentaries. I. Sullivan, Anita. II. Title.

BS1485.52 G66 2015

Manufactured in the U.S.A.   04/02/2015

Scripture quotations marked (NRSV) are taken from the New Revised Standard Version Bible, copyright 1989, Division of Christian Education of the National Council of the Churches of Christ in the United States of America. Used by permission. All rights reserved.

Scripture quotations marked (RSV) are taken from the Revised Standard Version of the Bible, copyright 1952 [2nd edition, 1971] by the Division of Christian Education of the National Council of the Churches of Christ in the United States of America. Used by permission. All rights reserved.

Scripture quotations marked (NJPS) are from the New Jewish Publication Society Version © 1985 by The Jewish Publication Society. All rights reserved.

To

Ralph Salisbury and Ingrid Wendt
dear friends and splendid poets

Contents

Preface | ix

1 Overture | 1
   Another Song of Songs Translation? | 1
   Solomon and the Song of Songs | 3
   The Song of Songs and Oral Poetry | 4
   The Song of Songs as a Book | 9
   Hebrew and Poetry | 12
   Some Other Works on the Song of Songs | 18
   Voices, Speakers, and "Authors" | 23
   The Arrangement of the Song of Songs | 26
   "Codes" in the Song of Songs | 27
   Translating Hebrew | 30
   Interpretive Essays | 32
   The Book's Arrangement | 33

2 The Song of Songs That Are Solomon's | 35
   Ch. 1:1 | 37
   Ch. 1:2–4 | 39
   Ch. 1:5–6 | 45
   Ch. 1:7–8 | 48
   Ch. 1:9—2:3 | 51
   Ch. 2:4–7 | 57
   Ch. 2:8–14 | 62
   Ch. 2:15–17 | 66
   Ch. 3:1–5 | 70
   Ch. 3:6–11 | 75
   Ch. 4:1–7 | 80
   Ch. 4:8 | 85
   Ch. 4:9–15 | 88
   Ch. 4:16—5:1 | 92
   Ch. 5:2—6:3 | 95
   Ch. 6:4–10 | 104
   Ch. 6:11–12 | 108
   Ch. 7:1–10 | 111
   A Brief Diversion on "Turn" | 118
   Ch. 7:11–14 | 120
   Ch. 8:1–4 | 123
   Ch. 8:5 | 126
   Ch. 8:6–7 | 129
   Ch. 8:8–10 | 137
   Ch. 8:11–14 | 140

3 Assisting with the Translation: A Contemporary Poet Takes a Look at an Old Poem—An Afterword / *Anita Sullivan* | 144

Bibliography | 151

Index | 153

Preface

EARLY IN MY CAREER on the faculty at Stanford University, I discovered that a whole world of literary work was to be done with the Hebrew Bible. I had to train myself to do it, assisted by much reading and much discussion with colleagues in departments of literatures in the University. Having now long qualified as a senior citizen among scholars of the Hebrew Bible, I may be mature enough to turn to the most interesting poetic source there, the Song of Songs. As the Preface is usually the last part of a book to be written, I can now say, having completed the work of the book except for final revisions, that I have greatly enjoyed a tour through a work that I have looked at for many years without publishing anything on it. One should not predict future intentions, though I have every intention of being present for a long time to come, whether or not I ever write anything more on the Hebrew Bible.

Several friends gave me essential assistance. Especially Rabbi Maurice Harris, who has himself published two books with Cascade Books, took over some editorial chores that required specific knowledge of the house's requirements of style and alleviated my time for more literary editing. I am most grateful to Rabbi Harris, and count his kindness as the beginning of a pleasant friendship.

I am pleased to include an Afterword written by Anita Sullivan, my wife and a published poet and writer. She gave me deep support during writing, commenting on the translations and the

Preface

essays in ways that have been extraordinarily helpful to the entire concept and performance. After most of the work was done, she composed the Afterword. It is a fine thing for the world and for husbands when wives contribute not only behind the scenes but also publicly available wisdom. Anita is a superb reader, writer, and translator, though of languages other than Hebrew, a profound critic of literature of all sorts, and in every sense a wise person. On reading her essay on the Song of Songs after I had finished several drafts of the book, I knew that the world should have it too. Her voice, far from being an echo, is a vigorous, lively, and independent presence.

Finally I bow deeply to the fine poets—none of them, as I think, known—who gave us the Song of Songs. It is no small thing to think, talk, write about love. That I spent so many years before coming to the Song gives me some sorrow at missed chances. But I would rather not think what a mess I likely would have made of it when I was a callow fifty or sixty. I am honored to be freed to think, read, and write with such delight about love, which I believe to be the supreme experience humans can have.

Edwin M. Good
Eugene, Oregon

1

Overture

Another Song of Songs Translation?

WELL, YES. IF I'M to discuss the book, I need to have a translation, as some readers will be unable to read it in Hebrew. If it is not an existing published one it must be one I have made myself. The only translation that I can decide to change if I need to and that is likely to agree with all (or most) of my views will be mine.

And why is it necessary to write about the Song of Songs? Are there not many fine studies, scholarly or not? Of course there are, but mine differs, being mine, from the others. No scholar can resist thinking that his or her account of a subject needs a book (or an article) to give readers the truth available in it. I have wanted for some time to think newly about the Song of Songs.

One of those thoughts has to do with a question of oral composition, transmission, and collection of the book. I suspect that, apart from the peculiarities of my translations and interpretations of the poems, including the analyses by which I have decided to separate poems from one another, the question of oral backgrounds is the point at which my discussion of it most differs from my predecessors. It may also be the most productive of disagreement—or, as one might more deeply wish, of discussion.

The Song of Songs

The modern scholarship of the Hebrew Bible, beginning from the later eighteenth century, has been focused almost entirely on written texts, how they were written, by whom, and for what intellectual purposes. During the 1950s and later, Scandinavian scholarship was interested in orality, no doubt because of the importance of oral epics and poetry in the Scandinavian traditions. My growing interest in the subject led to a too-brief visit on a sabbatical leave to Uppsala, Sweden, where I was able to meet some of the scholars at the university who were working on oral projects, including Ivan Engnell (1906–1964), the leading figure of the movement, to learn enough Swedish to be able to read some of their works available only in that language, and to begin acquaintance with the methods of study involved in the questions of orality. Apart from an article on the book of Hosea that I wrote in Uppsala, I have not returned to the subject seriously until now.

What I am able to do is limited. I cannot propose original states of the poems. We have only the final forms—except for some repetitions of parts of poems, such as references to gazelles and deer, usually together, and a repeated formula about a group under oath about its relation to love. There are no existing earlier versions, before the repeated revisions, retellings, and modifications that occurred in transmission and the collecting processes. One must assume that changes took place between the first and later oral versions, but they cannot be reconstructed. Second, there are two poetic narratives about a woman going out into Jerusalem in search of her lover, one more extensive than and rather different from the other. We are stuck with what happened to be the last forms recorded, and fortunately they are beautiful. These are the kinds of phenomena that students of orality look for to identify possible oral backgrounds.

Moreover, after having decided for myself about the places where one poem ended and another began, I began to notice words and similarities of sounds among words toward the ends of many poems that were repeated or imitated toward the beginnings of the next poems. They looked to me like linking words, perhaps aids to the memories of reciters or singers about which poem or song came next. Coming after I had concluded where poems ended and other poems began, this observation was not a method by which I separated poems from each other, but it seems now to be a way by which separate poems might originally have been placed together in the oral collecting process.

Some extremely fine studies of the Song, including the one by J. Cheryl Exum that I identify below as the best book available on the Song, have concluded that the book is a single poem, not a collection of several. Well, a high opinion of someone's work does not require that one agree with all of it—a fact to be expected of my book as well.

Solomon and the Song of Songs

English traditionally titles the book either "Song of Songs" or "Song of Solomon." That duplicity poses more than one further implication of the title: perhaps that Solomon was the author of the poems, or that they have importantly to do with him. The Hebrew title, Ch. 1:1, is discussed in more detail below at pp. 37–38, where the main portion of the book begins. A phrase in that title, *liš^{e}lomoh*, can be translated somewhat literally "to Solomon," "by Solomon," "owned by Solomon," or "connected with Solomon." He is mentioned several times in the book as a character or as an iconic figure, and we can assume that the name refers to the only Solomon in the Hebrew Bible, the second king of Israel, the son of David. His death in about 925 BCE sent the nation into a brief civil war, resulting in the permanent split of the twelve tribes into two nations, Israel in the north, Judah in the south. Solomon stands in Israel's history for the most luxurious kingship, the most extensive harem, the construction of the most impressive buildings, including the Jerusalem Temple, and remarkable wisdom. There are some indications, including the revolt at his death, that he was perceived by his nation as sometimes excessive. A remarkable biography of Solomon, not only while he was alive but also throughout the tradition after his death, is Steven Weitzman's, *Solomon: The Lure of Wisdom* (see Bibliography). I recommend it enthusiastically as a very inventive application of the idea of biography, extending to the subject's continuing presence in the culture long after his death.

As for Solomon's authorship, 1 Kgs 5:12 (English numbering 4:32) states that he composed three thousand proverbs and 1,005 songs (or poems). From that remark come the traditions that he was the author of the books of Proverbs and the Song of Songs. The tradition also names him the author of Qoheleth (English title, Ecclesiastes), reflecting the tradition of his wisdom. Besides these, a later book, the Wisdom of Solomon, is included in the Old Testament canons of Roman Catholic and Eastern Orthodox churches,[1] and among the Apocrypha (books understood as not quite canonical scripture) of some Protestant churches. Two other books of lesser reputation and dated early in the Common Era are the *Psalms of Solomon* and the *Odes of Solomon*, both written in Greek, the latter possibly a Christian book. Neither made it into any canonical biblical list. Only Proverbs, the Song of Songs, and Qoheleth are present in the Hebrew Bible. I must make clear that I do not believe that Solomon was actually the author of any of them. All contain instances of Hebrew vocabulary considerably later than 925 BCE, which points to continuing composition after Solomon had stopped writing or otherwise using words.

The Oral and the Song of Songs

Interested as I am in oral composition and transmission in the ancient Near East, I am fascinated by the way 1 Kgs 5:12 describes Solomon's authorships. The Hebrew text says not that Solomon "wrote" or "composed" proverbs and songs, but that he "spoke" them. That tradition allows a conclusion that the proverbs and songs came not from his writing hand but from his mouth, and I am interested in the thought that Solomon might have been unable to read or write. I see indications in the Song of Songs of transmission and collection by oral means, and I will point them out as we come to them in my essays on the individual poems. It is

---

1. Weitzman, *Solomon*, 75. Some other sources do not list Wisdom of Solomon in the Orthodox canon.

more difficult to find indications that the poems themselves were composed and/or transmitted by the oral means of recitation or singing, but I will search for such possibilities. The search is complicated, even compromised, by the fact that no earlier versions of the book exist for our comparisons.

Since the discovery—I call it that, not supposition or assumption—in the last century that the *Iliad* and *Odyssey* of Homer were composed and performed orally a long time before they were written down, a great deal of work has been done on other ancient literatures and the question of orality. Most of that work has centered on epics, many of them poetic like the Homeric ones, and other works of narrative poetry. The only other work on orality with respect to the kind of lyric poetry represented by the Song of Songs is a chapter in Albert B. Lord's posthumous book, *The Singer Resumes the Tale*. Chapter 2, "Oral Traditional Lyric Poetry," (pp. 22–68), deals entirely with South Slavic lyric poems and is based almost entirely on observations of repetitions from one poem to another. Fortunately, he was able to work with oral poetry still in living memory and in multiple versions. I mentioned above signs of what I think is orality, especially in the relations among the separate poems in the *Song*, and in repetitions of phrases from one poem to another as well as some poems that may be revised and altered versions of other poems in the book. The processes by which this poetry was composed, transmitted, performed, revised, and collected together are concealed in the long centuries when all of that was happening. We now have only the outcome of those events.

I admit that I cannot prove oral origins or transmissions of these poems. Scholars are supposed to accomplish that goal in order to make scholarly claims. I think I see indications but not sufficient evidence to claim the truth of the matter. Thinking about it, I found some remarks by and about a modern Hungarian poet that are worth including. Sándor Kányádi (b. 1929), remarks in a book, *In Contemporary Tense* (2013)[2] that, giving a reading of poems in a Romanian village, he asked a question of a little schoolboy: "What

---

2. Reviewed by Lénárt-Cheng in the Internet edition of *Rattle for the 21st Century*.

do you think a poem is?" The boy answered, "A poem is something that you have to tell." Kányádi remarked that he had been "brushed by a breeze coming from the beginning of time." A poem must be told. Homer knew that, the Romanian schoolboy knew it.

It is a complex statement. "Something that you have to tell" can mean several things. You have to tell it in contrast to reading or writing it. And who has to tell it? The poet? Anyone who hears it? Anyone who reads it, memorizes it? The reviewer of the book suggests that all those things are different from telling. She also insists that telling must be oral, and that the boy may have thought that "had to tell" referred both to the poet and to whoever came into contact with the poem. You and I must *tell* the poems we hear and read. But sometimes it is necessary to tell them by the somewhat inferior means of writing. I wish I could hear a poet speak—tell—these poems in Song of Songs in the language in which they came to be, so that I could get a sense of the sounds they intended to lay upon the world. I am a musician, for whom the most important thing that happens in the world is sound. Unfortunately, classical Hebrew is a dead language, at least in terms of the actual sounds it made. We know the sounds Hebrew makes now, but no language maintains its sounds intact for two thousand and more years. Meanwhile, we can only guess at how these poems might have sounded in the telling—or the singing. What were the rhythms of song or speech? And what the melodies of speech (which we think of as inflection—one does not speak in a monotone) and song?

You are perfectly at liberty to believe the numbers of Solomon's proverbs and songs given in 1 Kings and the decrees of tradition as to authorships. Like most modern scholars, I do not believe any of it, any more than I believe that King David wrote the Psalms that are credited to him in the Bible. That does not mean that those who made these authorial ascriptions were telling lies, which are falsehoods that their tellers know are false. The ancients surely wanted all of these things to be true and may well have thought that they were. Ascribing all of these books to Solomon was no doubt a way of raising them in the Jewish consciousness in the late centuries up to the Common Era, and I hold these authorial identifications to be mainly responsible for the presence in the Hebrew Bible of Proverbs, Song of Songs, and Qoheleth, and of the Wisdom of Solomon in Roman Catholic and Orthodox Bibles and among the Apocrypha of some Protestant churches. The Jews wished to enshrine their heroes in what became the sacred book, as the tradition enshrined Moses as the author of Genesis–Deuteronomy, an ascription of which I am equally dubious. Or the prophetic anthology of Isaiah in its sixty-six chapters. It is not believable, and so we have the necessary fictions of "Second" Isaiah (chs. 40–55) and "Third" Isaiah (chs. 56–66), based on the persuasive indications of times and situations different from those faced by Isaiah himself. The earliest claims that such works came from the original named prophet cannot be found. I suspect that at least some of them came to the fore not long before the beginning of the Common Era, but I cannot prove that opinion.

If it had been important to anyone, I suspect that Solomon's authorship would have turned up in the famous remark about the Song of Songs ascribed to Rabbi Akiva in the first half of the second century of the Common Era: "Heaven forbid that any man in Israel has ever doubted that the Song of Songs defiles the hands, for the entire world is not worth the day on which the Song of Songs was written; for all the writings are holy, but the Song of Songs is the holy of holies." Landy quotes the statement in Hebrew.[3] To "defile the hands," or "make the hands unclean" is a rabbinical definition of canonical status, as the rules required that touching any part of any canonical (by definition holy) book be preceded and immediately followed by washing the hands, because holiness makes you dangerous to yourself and others. The scribes who copied biblical manuscripts spent a great deal of time over the washbasin both before and after work.

Some scholars think that Akiva was among the first to propose allegory as the meaning of the Song, but, if so, this remark has nothing to do with it. It is a very forthright argument against a view that must have circulated at Akiva's time that the Song of

---

3. Landy, *Paradoxes of Paradise*, 13.

Songs ought not to be in the biblical canon. Clearly Akiva centers on that point: "all the writings are holy." It is not clear whether "the writings" means the entire biblical canon or the third section of it called "Writings" (*Ketuwbiym*), which includes Psalms, Proverbs, Job, Qoheleth, Song of Songs, and a number of other books of various kinds. (The first section of the canon is the Torah, that is the Pentateuch, Genesis to Deuteronomy, and the second is the Prophets, which includes the historical books Joshua through Kings, and the usual prophetic books, Isaiah to Malachi.) But surely Akiva was arguing not that Solomon wrote the Song or that it is an allegory, but that the Song is properly canonical, using the analogy of its title to the definition in the Torah of the tabernacle and later of the secret place in the Temple where only the High Priest went as the "holy of holies," "the most holy place." So not only is the date of its writing, in Akiva's view, worth more than any other day since the Creation, but the book is holy in terms of place—and books are places, among other things—in comparison to the holiest place in the Temple. Of course, the Temple had been destroyed, along with its "holy of holies," some years before by the Romans. So as Akiva saw it, the Bible and the Song of Songs took the religious place that the Temple had occupied. It's hard to conceive a more central position in Judaism.

Those who are familiar with the Hebrew Bible are sometimes at a loss to comprehend the presence there of a book of erotic poetry. It is at least a very different kind of presentation from the usual biblical views of the relations of men and women. This is surely the reason that medieval theologians proposed that the book was an allegory of love between God and the Jewish people or the Christian Church. Not that the Hebrew Bible condemns human sexuality, unlike later Christian traditions of the importance of celibacy and of ambiguities about the morality of sexual activity. Akiva, to be sure, does not define what constitutes being holy; he attests to its presence. And the Song certainly does not inculcate celibacy—some English bishops of an earlier age blamed its presence in Bibles for the corruption of Anglican choir-boys: they were reading the Song instead of paying attention to the sermon.

Perhaps Solomon's reputation as a lover had some influence on the thought that he composed the Song of Songs.

The Song of Songs as a Book

We start with my conclusion that this is a book of poems—some scholars think it is a single poem—that focus on youthful love. It is a book of love poems, and in classical Hebrew the word *šiyr* meant both "poem" and "song."

It was not the first such book in the ancient world, and certainly not the last, but is the only collection of its kind that survived in classical Hebrew. There are imitations of and allusions to love poems in some of the prophetic poetry (for instance, Isa 5:1–7 and the Book of Hosea). Several papyri contain splendid ancient Egyptian love poems, and some survived also from Sumerian and Akkadian sources in Mesopotamian cuneiform tablets, not to ignore those from classical Greece. Many of the Near Eastern ones are certainly earlier than the Song of Songs, and there was a long tradition later of love poems in Arabic, some before and many after the rise of Islam.

I suppose that the Song came to its final form (the limits to that I will shortly note) at some time about the third or second century (300–100) BCE. Some scholars have noticed traces of even later Hebrew vocabulary; see especially C. and A. Bloch, *The Song of Songs*,[4] for a rather long list of apparently later words. Some still want to date it earlier. Robert Alter mentions that some scholars put its completion early in "the First Commonwealth period," but he never says just when he thinks that was.[5] When was it composed? I say "composed," not "written," because I suspect that most, and conceivably all, of these poems originated in oral form. I know of no way to demonstrate that thought or to single out even an approximate date when some of the poems were first heard. Solomon's presence in the texts is important only because he is mentioned in it, mostly

---

4. Bloch and Bloch, *The Song of Songs*, 24.
5. Alter, *The Art of Biblical Poetry*, 185.

as a distant character. The poems that mention him probably came into being well after 925 BCE, and it is worth saying that that makes those poems fiction. Love poetry is, perhaps of all poetry, the least dependent for style and subject matter on historical contexts, unless combined with mention of other issues like known authorship, war, or natural calamities. The text of the Song of Songs does not help us in that respect to date its origin.

The book surely went through a long series of compilations before the final one(s). And once written it was always copied by hand until—and even after—the invention of printing in about 1450 CE in Mainz, Germany. The complete Hebrew Bible first appeared in print in 1488 in Soncino, Italy. So we are looking, as my suggested date of final composition proposes, at about 1,600 years of hand-copying and very probably more, perhaps many centuries more. Anyone who has tried to copy by hand a text that was written by hand has had the experience of making mistakes. The scribes were very careful and under great limitations and rules, but mistakes certainly happened in the Song of Songs. Not many of them, and probably only one that made some words incomprehensible: see 6:12. Meanwhile, of course, the Hebrew Bible was translated into Greek and Latin more than once, and from there into other languages, all in hand copies and in many different scripts and translations. It entered a number of languages, such as Aramaic, Coptic, Ethiopic, Arabic, Persian, Georgian, and Armenian, as well as some less prominent ones, and later into more modern languages. Those translations sometimes provide information that has been used by scholars to correct what seem errors in the Hebrew. More persuasively, they show how variable the traditions of biblical books became as they were transferred into other languages and cultures.

The Hebrew of the manuscripts consisted entirely of consonants. Systems of vowel marks were invented only in the Middle Ages. Of course, the spoken language had vowels in it. They just were not written. Think a little about that. Suppose we wrote English only in consonants: *spps w wrt nglsh nl n cnsnnts. Myb t wld hv bn rltvly sy, bt nthr sntnc mght b hrdr.* Did you figure out what that says? Some "words" could be read in more than one way, and many of the ancient manuscripts did not even put spaces between words. *Thtwldmkrdngtvnhrdr.* Various systems of vowel marks were developed for Hebrew, and only at about 1000 CE was a system practically unanimously adopted: the so-called ben-Asher vocalization system, following a slightly earlier one called ben-Naphtali, which used the same principles but different details. Ben-Asher's system consists of dots and lines below, above, or within the consonant signs, and other signs indicating patterns of chanting, which combined with accents show how the biblical text was read and chanted in medieval synagogues. Manuscripts of the Torah (Genesis–Deuteronomy) intended for reading in synagogue services continue to be hand-copied without vowels.

All of that puts about 1,200 years between the assumed completion of the consonantal text of the Song and the first additions of vowel signs to Hebrew manuscripts. 1,200 years is a long time for language changes, especially combined with movements of Jews away from Palestine into other countries, most notably southwestern and northern Europe. The Hebrew spoken and chanted in European or even Near Eastern communities and their synagogues in the eleventh century CE was a different language from the one spoken and sung in Palestine in the third–second centuries BCE.

Our major problem is that our knowledge of how the earlier Hebrew was pronounced is very limited. In the Middle Ages several different traditions of pronouncing Hebrew arose, the Ashkenazic tradition in northern Europe, especially in Poland and Germany, the Sephardic in Spain and southern Europe, and others in the Near East. Those traditions were heavily influenced by the languages around them. A form that combined German and Hebrew known as Yiddish (properly Jüdisch Deutsch–Jewish German) was a central factor in Germany, and the presence of Arabs in Spain made the Sephardic Hebrew more closely related to spoken Arabic, but also influenced by Spanish. In fact, a medieval Spanish Muslim thinker, Ibn Arabi, wrote love poems in Arabic not at all dissimilar to the Song of Songs, and Jewish writers in Spain sometimes wrote their books in Arabic. Maimonides, perhaps the greatest of them, wrote his famous *Guide for the Perplexed*, a work that is still studied, in Arabic. A somewhat modernized form of Ashkenazic Hebrew is the major language now in use in Israel, as well as in most American synagogues.

Hebrew and Poetry

One of the characteristics of this publication is that I have given the Hebrew text of the poems in Hebrew characters of the entire text, as well as translation into English. I do that not with the expectation that every reader will closely examine the Hebrew text. I know perfectly well that few will know enough Hebrew to make much if any sense of it. Most will know no Hebrew at all. So why is the Hebrew there?

The reason is simple. I want readers to be constantly reminded that the book they are reading about is an old Hebrew book, which has suffered one more translation into English. That does not make the Song an English book. It is and always will be a Hebrew book, at least 2000 years old. The Hebrew text is there to remind readers of the fact that it is a Hebrew book. It was not written for us but for them. We have inherited it through Christianity or Judaism (or both), and we have been bidden by both to read it. We may wonder when we read it why we are expected to, because it is pure love poetry and—I will argue—it has nothing to do with religion, Christian, Jewish or other. It is poetry of human love, the sort of which most of us have some experience. The point, however, is not to worry about reading the Hebrew, just to be aware that it is there and to think occasionally why it is there.

Losing the knowledge of Hebrew pronunciation affects poetry, of course, more than prose. Poetry involves rhythm, relations among sounds, especially but not only consonants, and inflections and accents (melodic patterns, if you like). Poetries in all languages have such patterns, which, of course, differ markedly from one language to another and from one period in a language to another. If you have ever tried to read Chaucer's *Canterbury Tales* in the original form (Chaucer died in about 1400 CE) or have heard

Overture

someone read it aloud, you will know something of the problem, and his English is only 600-plus years old. Closer to the problem with the Song is *Beowulf*, thought to have been composed in the 700s CE, perhaps about as far from us as the Song was from the first use of vowels in the Hebrew text. And though *Beowulf* is Old English, it must be translated to be at all intelligible to modern speakers of English.

With Hebrew, the frustration of uncertainty about how the language sounded in its originating times has no solution, except guessing. I am certain, from examining a good number of poems in the Hebrew Bible over the years, that some of what Europeans tend to think about poetry is simply not present in the Hebrew works.

Even the awareness that there is poetry in the Bible was a long time in coming. The King James Version (1611) printed the entire English Bible as prose, with each numbered verse occupying a separate paragraph. That includes the Psalms, the Proverbs, Job, and the Song of Songs—all mostly poetry as we now know and leaving out a great deal of other poetry more recently identified, especially in the prophets, as well as poems that turn up within narrative texts. The King James translators probably did not know, or at least made no effort to show, that any of these books are poetry, perhaps their only literary failing. That translation well deserves the term applied to it in a famous article by John Livingston Lowes titled "The Noblest Monument of English Prose." And we should pay close attention to the word "prose."

The modern discovery of poetry in the Bible can be laid at the door of Bishop Robert Lowth (1710–1787) in England, who, on being named Professor of Poetry at Oxford, presented a series of lectures, later published in Latin and English as *De sacra poesi Hebraeorum* (1753; English trans., *On the Sacred Poetry of the Hebrews*, 1815). Lowth demonstrated the presence of poetry not only in the Psalms and such places, but also in the prophets. There is rather ambiguous indication in earlier Greek and Latin works, that some thinkers realized that the Hebrew Bible contained poetry. St. Jerome, translating from Hebrew into Latin, mentioned in some of his essays that some passages revealed an equivalent of certain

Latin metres. Well, that was wishful thinking, but the perception in the Roman Empire of the fourth century CE that there was poetry in Hebrew is extremely interesting.

We have been used to thinking in English about regular metrical rhythms (as Jerome was), though much modern English poetry has departed from the schemes of meter. Hebrew poetry does not have meter, certainly not in the too rigid patterns of accented and non-accented syllables that some English poetry has traditionally used: "This is the forest primeval, the murmuring pines and the hemlocks." It is awfully difficult to say Longfellow's words without accenting the first of every three syllables, and that jiggy dactylic rhythm is a mark, even in English, of less than splendid poetry. On the other hand, no decent actor playing Hamlet would speak "To be or not to be, that is the question," accenting only the syllables that strict iambic pentameter would designate: "be—not—be—is—ques." Shakespeare doubtless wrote what can be called "iambic pentameter," but flexible rhythm is part of what makes his poetry superlative.

There seems in Hebrew verse to be a preponderance of two, three, or four words in a poetic line, and most Hebrew words now have one accent, but there are no frequent and identifiable rhythmic patterns of accents and non-accents, nor does Hebrew poetry use rhyme. In any case we are mostly ignorant of Hebrew pronunciation in the ancient period. The vowels, some consonants, and accentuations provided in the printed biblical Hebrew text are medieval, not ancient, and they must have differed in good part from when this poetry was in its maturity, let alone in its infancy, perhaps eight or nine centuries before the Song of Songs was written down.

The Song of Songs was probably one of the later biblical books to be completed in something like its present form. The problem is even greater with earlier books, and with survivals of really early poems, such as the Song of Deborah (Judges 5) and other poems doubtless composed orally and in folk settings. Such problems have led some very fine scholars to give up on any effort to restore poetry to its original forms.

Overture

A considerable amount of study of ancient Hebrew poetry has taken place since Lowth's contribution. I consider the best general treatment of the subject to be Robert Alter's (see Bibliography). His book has been influential for the excellent reason that it rests on impeccable scholarship and uses language that is understandable and clear. Especially helpful for our purposes is his chapter 8, "The Garden of Metaphor," which gives to the Song of Songs itself an insightful discussion of how poetry works in the book, and particularly how the rich effusion of metaphors can be understood.[6] Alter has not always had his way with scholars, and I think it valuable to mention also James L. Kugel, *The Idea of Biblical Poetry: Parallelism and Its History* (see Bibliography). Kugel's subtitle demonstrates his particular interest in parallelism and how poetry is related to prose. He finds parallelisms in prose passages as well as in poetry, and it cannot therefore be the exclusive property of poetry. He thinks that poetry is a kind of speech very like prose but at the formal edge of it.

Bishop Lowth first showed the centrality in classical Hebrew poetry of "parallelism," or, to use his Latin phrase, *parallelismus membrorum*, "parallelism of the members" (or parts). He saw the basic type to be a two-part sentence, in which the two parts (members) of the statement were organized in parallel. He found three kinds of parallelisms: "synonymous parallelism," where the second part in effect repeats what the first said but in different words; "antithetic parallelism," in which the second part reverses the statement of the first. The third kind he called "synthetic parallelism," and in effect, it is not parallel at all. For instance, "Your cheeks are lovely with pendants, / your neck with necklaces" (Song 1:10) displays Lowth's synonymous parallelism: the two phrases in effect say something close to the same thing, and there are specific parallel terms between them: "cheeks" and "neck," "pendants" and "necklaces." I find no antithetic parallelism in the Song of Songs; an example is Prov 14:20: "A pauper is despised even by his peers, / but a rich man has many friends." "Pauper" and "rich man" are antithetical, as are "despised" and "friends." Proverbs is especially

6. Alter, *The Art of Biblical Poetry*, 185–203.

rich in antithetic parallelism. The synthetic is not difficult to find: "Why should I be covered up / beside your friends' flocks?" (Song 1:7). The second line simply continues the sentence of the first, and that seems to me not to be parallel at all. But apparently, Bishop Lowth wished everything to be called parallel, so he even thought of a parallel term for a non-parallel couplet.

The matter has been considerably complicated beyond the Bishop's three categories. We will see some very distinctive kinds of parallelisms in the *Song*, which do not quietly nestle into Lowth's types, and which are often extraordinarily subtle. I will pay special attention to noticing them as we go through the poems. Moreover, in the Song, we often have to deal with poetic units in three lines, tercets (or triplets) as distinguished from couplets, an issue with which Lowth did not grapple. A third line adds serious complication. For instance, the third line of the concluding tercet of what I identify as the first poem, Song 1:4c-e, does not fit any pattern, Lowth's or any other:

> joyous and happy,   we celebrate your loving, better than wine;
>
> they are right to love you.

The opening couplet is a somewhat loose instance of synonymous parallelism, but the third line, though it uses a synonym of "loving" in the second, also has a different subject, "they," instead of "we," and, in fact, it echoes a line earlier in the poem: "and so girls love you." Tercets simply wipe away the structure of Lowth's discovery. The poetry has parallelism, but it is much more complex than the simplicities of his schemes of couplets. It is, however, important to recognize parallelism where it occurs, and to take account of more complexities in it than we might expect.

In working through a fine book on oral poetry, John Miles Foley, *How to Read an Oral Poem* (see Bibliography), I came to a sense of parallelism new for me. Discussing with some South Slavic oral poets who compose and sing epic poetry, Foley asked them about words. Their answer was remarkable: a "word" for them is not what

Overture

we think of—man, woman, house, wine, go, sing—but is, as one of the singers explained, the basic rhetorical units in the poem which might be a phrase of three words, a line of ten syllables (the traditional line in the epic poetry composed and sung in that language by men—women use lines of eight syllables), or even two or more lines, perhaps ten of what we would call "words." But the whole is the "word" as those poets understood it, if it is a basic rhetorical unit, and the poem is composed of many "words" of that sort.[7]

The thought struck me that we might, in the Song of Songs and other Hebrew poetry, take the units of parallelism or the similar units, sometimes not parallel, and some of the couplets and tercets—perhaps even larger groups of them—as the "words" that are the fundamental rhetorical units of the poetry. Hence, the oral compositions are not focused on the single words and combining them into phrases and lines, but the poets were thinking of whole lines and groups of lines, doubtless often familiarly traditional, and stringing them together into poems.

The South Slavic poets with whom Foley spoke, like Homer, composed epic-length narrative poems, and Foley confined his interest in the book to narrative poetry, especially epic, and very rarely touched on anything resembling lyric or love poetry. The poets of the Song composed, remembered, and revised shorter lyric poems. But the process of thinking of their "words" instead of only our words comes out to the rhetoric of love songs. Students of oral poetry have done less work on lyric or love poetry than on narrative and especially epic poetry, though a great deal of lyricism is out there awaiting attention from (dare I call them?) oraliticians.

So this poetry has form, some of it relatively simple and some quite complicated. That such form was known and deliberately used seems to me self-evident. I see tercets carefully used to follow or precede couplets, and being themselves combined with other tercets or other combinations. For instance in Song 1:6, the third and last line shrewdly adds a completely new thought in the same image as the two preceding it. And the next poem, 1:7–8, is structured as speeches of the two characters, both in five-line stanzas.

---

7. Foley, *How to Read an Oral Poem*, 11–21.

Her speech, 1:7, is a tercet followed by a couplet, and his, 1:8, is a couplet followed by a tercet. Such symmetry can hardly be accidental. These were sophisticated poets in a sophisticated tradition, even if we call it a "folk" tradition. Nor does such sophistication require that a poem possess from the outset only one poet.

Lowth's identification of Hebrew poetry in two-line units has caused some scholars, who apparently lacked poetic imagination to refuse to recognize tercets. I have seen scholarly works on poetic Hebrew that simply emended away all third lines in a poem. They weren't supposed to be there, and therefore the scholar took it on himself to "correct" them. Scholars can sometimes be so unscholarly! I take the view that my job is not to rewrite the poetry but to come as close as I can to understanding it. At the same time, we sometimes must recognize errors in the transmission of the poems over those many centuries.

Errors in copying that happened hundreds of years ago can make understanding difficult, and I prefer not to correct such errors when they involve consonants. I have broken my own rule once in the poetry that follows. In 3:10 is the phrase "by the daughters of Jerusalem," in which "by" (Hebrew *min* acting as a prefix to "daughters") completely messes up what would be a simple if rather ordinary parallel couplet. I omitted the consonant from the text to make that couplet. Such breaches of stated intention must be admitted. Otherwise, if I simply cannot make sense of something, I leave blanks in the translation with notes explaining why I do that. The only instance of such a case in the Song is at 6:12. Vowel mistakes, on the other hand, are fair game, because they can't be assumed to be from the biblical period in any case.

Some Other Works on the Song of Songs

A great deal of ink has been sprayed across the world about the Song of Songs. I must first mention the book that seems to me the best work I have ever seen on it: J. Cheryl Exum, *Song of Songs: A Commentary* (see Bibliography). Professor Exum is a friend from a good many years back, and her book turns out to be the principal

Overture

foil upon which I have written mine. Indeed, I think of my book as in important ways a colloquy with hers, as will be shown by the number of citations to her in my notes. It is not that I agree with everything she says, as she knows and will recognize. My principal disagreement lies in her conclusion that the book is a single poem, divided into some parts, where I find it an anthology of separate poems, related by style and theme and perhaps by characters. Disagreements among scholars (and among friends) often do not represent divisions but rather connections, even discussions. I have shamelessly snapped up many of Professor Exum's solutions to problems we both recognize, and I have not always acknowledged it. I strongly recommend that readers of my book read hers. It is much longer than mine, splendidly written, subtly and clearly argued, scholarship at its very best. On only two matters may it be said that either she is or I am "wrong." One is the question already noted, whether the book is one poem or an anthology of several poems (twenty-three in my opinion). The other is my interest in trying to trace evidence of orality in the poems, an interest that she has told me she does not share.

I have followed Professor Exum's example in one particular. She inserts the identities of the speakers in each section, and I have done the same with the separate poems, and, where it applies, within poems that are dialogues. The Hebrew texts of the poems do not make these identifications. I find three speakers in the book: a woman, whom I identify as "she," a man, whom I name "he," and a group of women referred to as "Jerusalem's daughters." In a few places I find myself unable to identify anyone (or group) as the speaker. On those poems I have noted "speaker unknown" or have put question marks where the speaker should be noted. "Jerusalem's daughters" function in some ways as a chorus, and they are to be found especially in connection with the woman, seemingly as a group of her familiar friends. "Daughters" is a general term for "women" (every woman is, of course, someone's daughter) and some poems refer in parallel to men as "sons"—similarly every man is a son. "Jerusalem," of course, is the ancient city itself, a metaphorical "mother" of the daughters.

The Song of Songs

Much of the book seems to take place in Jerusalem. Ancient cities were never large as we think of large cities and were much closer to the rural areas around them than are our monstrous modern metropolises. So the characters in the book are often out in the country, and we should not think of city parks or anything like them. The characters are for the most part young people, perhaps younger than we would instinctively think of them.

Whether the woman and the man who speak here are always the same persons cannot be answered with certainty. I see no reason in the style of the poetry to think of either as more than one personality, but I cannot rule out the thought. Indeed, Francis Landy[8] argues that these two characters are not really characters in the sense of identifiable personalities, but are rather "images of the poet." I am not sure whether he means that they are "images" that the poet used or are images that depict the poet. The idea that one poet might have both male and female "images" in both senses is not to be dismissed. He speaks of a singular "poet," and of that I am quite dubious. If this is an anthology of poems, it does not matter to me whether "she" or "he" is always the same person. If they are sometimes not the same, that may add persuasion to my supposition of multiple but not identifiable "poets" working with and against each other over centuries of composition in speech or writing, performance in song or recitation, revision by performers, listeners, and scribes, and the processes of collection and selection.

In some ways, thinking of the book as a single poem must in some sense entail conceiving of its author as a single person or, perhaps, as a last editor. If, however, the book made its way through centuries, during which it was recited, adapted, revised, spoken, sung, perhaps sometimes partially or completely reconceived, then there is no point in trying to find an "author." I think of it as the outcome of a long process of composition involving what might well be a very large number of composers, many of whom left their footprints, but not in ways that allow us to identify them or even to be certain that they are different.

---

8. Landy, *Paradoxes of Paradise*, 62.

Overture

I am more nearly persuaded than I was on beginning this project that the Song was written down only near the very end of the process, and that the poems were conceived and reconceived for centuries (how many?). Nor was the writing the end of the changes, but copying, repeated reading, and translation produced still other modifications and interpretations. Perhaps the most important later interpretive shift was the determination in Late Antiquity and the Middle Ages that the Song was an allegory. Jewish interpreters then came to read it as referring not to human love but to the love between God and Israel, and Christians saw it as meaning the love between Christ or God and the Church. The allegorical interpretations allowed the book full religious presence in the Bible and decidedly set aside the textures of love poetry in their usual applications.

I do not know any contemporary work on the Song of Songs that seriously takes it as an allegory, theological or other. David Carr, *The Erotic Word: Sexuality, Spirituality, and the Bible* (see Bibliography) seems to me to come closer to it than anyone else, and he may well be annoyed to read that. There is more theology in Carr's book as I read it than in most, and certainly much more than in mine. Perhaps I should not confuse theology and allegory by lumping them together. At the same time, I perceive divine names in the text of chapter 8:6–7 that he passes over without mention. Exum sees them too, but thinks they are not being used as divine names.[9]

For all of those reasons, it seems to me that the book is the product of so many "authors" over so many centuries, including the allegorical interpreters, that identifying any of them is simply unthinkable. In this, I disagree with Francis Landy, who discusses what "the poet" did, thought, knew. But Landy is right, as is Exum, in identifying the book as of human authorship. In that, they—and I—differ from Rabbi Akiva, who implicitly thought of its author as divine.

I imagine, without being able to prove it, long times of recitation, singing, listening, revising, sometimes done on the spur of

---

9. Carr, *The Erotic Word*, 135; Exum, *Song of Songs*, 253.

the moment in a performance. I suppose that the process changed words and forms of the poems to replace earlier forms and texts. I have referred to some patterns of forms, and they may have been part of the processes of revision. The earlier versions have not survived where we can find them, though they might have remained for a time in other locations. Some of the repetitions in the book itself may reflect multiple transmissions, and I will later discuss an instance that looks as if it may be two different versions of what might have begun as one poem.

The book, whether a single poem or many, is the product of a whole culture at work on a subject that whole cultures ponder: the remarkable fact that men and women love each other—not always, as we can see everywhere around us. Many cultures know both love that happens between men and women and between men only and women only, as well as love's own opposite. Those other directions the *Song* does not take.

Men and women in various cultures express their love for each other in many varying ways. But every culture spends a great deal of energy thinking about love and living it. I propose that this wonderfully variable group of poems was the product of more minds, loves, and time than we can imagine. What is most wonderful about it is that it seems unitary enough for some readers to find it a single poem with, presumably, a single author—at least, a single *final* author.

A superbly crafted book on the whole matter of an oral background is Susan Niditch, *Oral World and Written Word: Ancient Israelite Literature* (see Bibliography). Professor Niditch deals only with narrative literature (leaving poetry—unknowingly—to me). But her sense of the Israelite tradition is nearly identical to mine. She portrays it as one in which most members of the culture received their knowledge of its cultural goods, its songs, stories, laws, rituals, history, through their ears, not their eyes, by hearing it told, recited, sung, not by reading it. Though ancient Israel wrote what has been called, not quite accurately, an alphabet, the notion that most Israelites could read seems to me quite mistaken. I wish I could go into the entire question of oral poetry with the care and precision with which Prof. Niditch has gone into Israelite narrative. But I have come to a point of seeing limitations of time and of energy to accomplish all that I would like to do. Unless I can live to about 107 years of age, with full vigor, a condition I cannot imagine is really thinkable, completing that project is likely not possible. Perhaps a reader whom I do not know will snatch up the banner I hold out and dash away with it. I would dearly love to live long enough to read the resulting work.

I have also pondered whether earlier or later forms of at least some of the poems were composed by women. Did Israel know female poets as Greece knew Sappho and others? We simply do not know, though the "Song of Deborah" in Judges 5, claims that Deborah (and Barak) sang the song, which suggests that the tradition supposed Deborah had at least a hand (or a voice) in its first composition. After the crossing of the Sea at the Exodus, chapter 15, there is first a long poem that the text says was sung by Moses and the Israelites, followed by a much shorter one sung by Miriam and "the women" (vv. 20–21), which repeats the first lines of the longer song. Was the shorter version part of an original, and did Miriam and the women improvise it? In many cultures, victory songs at military success and laments, for example, were composed and sung by women. Other kinds of poetry are also known in various cultures to be improvised by women. In contemporary Afghanistan, groups of women get together to improvise, read, and hear each other's poetry, focused on their situations, as described in an article in the *New York Times*.[10]

Voices, Speakers, and "Authors"

All of that does not help in deciding who might have composed the *Song*'s poems in the voice of the woman, or of "Jerusalem's daughters." I sense that "she" speaks a kind of knowledge and truthfulness about a woman's approach to situations she experiences, and, though I continue to plead ignorance, the thought that those poems might have been composed by women is not difficult for me

---

10. Griswold, "Why Afghan Women Risk Death to Write Poetry."

to consider. Were the man's poems composed by a man? Perhaps. If men could compose poems in women's voices, doubtless women could compose poems in men's voices. On the other hand, given my view of these poems as oral and to some extent fluid in form and performance, there is no way to be sure of the gender of any poet. I find it much easier to suppose that they have been through so many voices and persons that they belong to the culture at large and to both sexes. In fact, you will see a number of poems in which the "woman" and the "man" discuss the subject. Can you imagine the fun poetic-minded people of both sexes might have had composing or revising poems like that in performance? To be sure, we must imagine the kinds of occasions for those performances. I do not recall any mentions of them in the Hebrew Bible.

I am willing to think that some of these poems could have been originally written. I have no candidates in mind; the thought is a tentative and theoretical one. Have I sufficiently made the case that ascription of the Song or any of its parts to Solomon is a late fiction from many centuries after he was no longer with us (except in Professor Weitzman's terms)? Whether readers are as persuaded of that as I am does not matter, and I will stop belaboring it.

The only other technical and theoretical issue to which I need to nod is the question of the Song of Songs as allegory. I referred to it above as an invention of the Middle Ages, and I believe it was, though there are some reasons to think allegory was first put forward in Late Antiquity. Allegory approaches literature as functioning simultaneously on two levels, ordinarily a basically literal level, where every-thing means just what it says, and a higher one where all the language implies a different subject. Perhaps the best-known English allegories are John Bunyan's *The Pilgrim's Progress* and *Gulliver's Travels* by Jonathan Swift. Pondering the Hebrew Bible over a good many years, I have never seen any indication that an allegorical approach to subjects was used or familiar in biblical Israel. I begin therefore by doubting that an original allegorical method of presentation in this poetry is at all likely. It's not that Israelite and ancient Near Eastern thinkers were slow-witted or intellectually incompetent. They worked with the intellectual tools that their periods, languages, and cultures familiarly used. Medieval Europe, on the other hand, ran to multiple simultaneous levels, resting on the philosophical tradition inherited from the Greeks. The Song, as you will observe, is full of metaphor, simile, and comparison, but it does not in my judgment entertain thoughts of overall simultaneous dualities of the thorough-going kinds on which allegory lives.

That there are, however, double meanings of words in the *Song* is not only certain but very much to be expected. I will not here discuss any particular instance of it, but I may mention my perception that the poem in 8:6–7 has some centrally important words with double meanings. Discussion of that is in the essay on that poem.

The allegorical approach to the Song leaps naturally from the absence of a deity in the poetry to the assumption that a holy book in Israel could not have omitted reference to the Israelite deity, and therefore it must be concealed as, for instance, divine instead of merely human love. So the lovers cannot be just boy and girl but must include the divine and the human. As I perceive the male and female in the *Song* as intellectually, socially, and amorously on the same level, I cannot go on to perceive that they reflect the kind of basic division between the divine and the human assumed by religion, medieval, earlier and later, and Jewish and Christian alike. The divine and the human in the Middle Ages were completely different from each other, and therefore allegorical thought, separating one set of understandings from another, naturally moved in to interpret. But we need to notice that in that kind of interpretation, the male character quite naturally assumes the role of the deity in the duality—and that too tells us much of what we need to know about medieval allegory. I do not suggest that the divine and the human were on levels of equality in the Hebrew Bible or in other ancient civilizations. But they did not apply their ideas of differences to simultaneous dualities of the sort that allegory requires, and in the Song, as I read it, the man especially is on no higher level of power or intellect than is the woman. Why should he, and how could he, represent the level of the divine? This equality of the man and the woman in the book was one of the major surprises that it sprang on me. Ancient Hebrew culture was very much male-centered, and its society left no doubt that power and authority resided in men, as even some dipping in the legal texts, for instance, will demonstrate. But when the Hebrews wrote poetry about love, men and women lived in equality.

I do not mean to refuse to the Song of Songs the presence of any kind of spirituality. The religious is not the only spiritual option available to the human mind, and surely one might—and I would—propose that love itself would qualify. On the whole, I do not find instances of what I would think of as "religious" spirituality in the Song. David Carr's, *The Erotic Word*, chapter 10 ("The Erotic and Mystical: Bringing Sexuality and Spirituality Together in Reading the Song of Songs"),[11] if I understand what I am reading, seems to regard the Song as belonging in the realm of Christianity, or at least to work toward such an end, and I have some difficulties with that idea. I think the spirituality that the Song presumes behind its every line is of a very different kind, where love is the highest value, over which no authority has power, and which does not recognize any element of physical suffering as part of its meaning. I incline against reading later spiritual forms, even Christian ones, into the Hebrew Bible. To do so, in my view, necessitates imposing later thoughts and ideas on earlier times. It is perhaps only truthfulness to say that I try very hard to keep my earlier allegiance to Christianity out of my perceptions of the thought and religion of the Hebrew Bible. As my scholarly intention is to present the Song of Songs in its own forms and suppositions, Christian spirituality has no part in that presentation. I require that of myself, admitting that there may remain in my mind, all below conscious awareness, some residue of that spirituality. But I speak of myself and make no such demand on others.

The Arrangement of the Song of Songs

As I noted earlier, I have identified the speakers whose voices are heard in these poems, as "she," "he," and "daughters." In one poem,

---

11. Carr, *The Erotic* Word, 119–51.

3:6–11, the speaker cannot be identified. It describes Solomon's coming with troops from the desert, and there I have noted the speaker as "unknown." In 7:1, the poem begins with a demand that a woman dancer "Turn," and a remark of hers in the next verse or so suggests that the first line is spoken by a group of men. Remarking earlier that I cannot make up my mind whether "she" and "he" are always the same persons, I leave the identities in those terms. It is important to identify them because English has some peculiarities that prevent our always knowing who is referred to by such pronouns as "you." Unlike English, Hebrew distinguishes those by gender and number, both in the pronouns themselves and in verbal forms. Where "you" has a masculine form in a poem spoken by the woman, it is the man, but if "you" is feminine plural, we can assume that it is the daughters, and in at least one instance, where the Hebrew pronoun is masculine plural, it is addressed to a group of men (3:3).

I have adopted the way Robert Alter presents the lines of poetry, where the second line of a couplet is placed at the right side of the page, beginning at the center. If there is a tercet, the third line is centered on a separate line, usually below the lines with which it belongs but in a few instances, such as 1:2, it precedes its related couplet. In difference from Alter, I refer to the single parts as "lines" and the couplets or tercets as "verses." He names as "line" what I call "verse," and as "verset" what I call "line." I have reproduced these line-patterns in the Hebrew texts.

"Codes" in the Song of Songs

By my sub-title I have placarded the term "code." It refers to a particular problem of ways in which these poems work. You will notice a number of recurring words, images, and ideas that are not instantly understandable to a modern reader. Not that we are ignorant of the referents of them. I think we understand something of the animals called "gazelles," "deer," and "foxes," for instance. We have certain suppositions about them, for example that gazelles are a type of antelope, graceful, slender, beautiful, and swift of foot, that deer are similar but not identical to gazelles, that foxes are shrewd and canny, and the like. What we do not know with any precision is how the ancient Hebrews thought of these animals, except from what they say about them—and that is not very extensive.

The foxes, we are told, ruin the vineyards, especially when they are in bloom. Exactly what that signifies is not clear, though there are indications from a good many areas of the world that foxes like grapes. Aesop wrote a fable about that in Greek. There are ways to understand what that poem (2:15) seems to mean, but the fact that the ruin of the vineyards takes place when the vines are blossoming rather than producing fruit makes it a bit more difficult. We will see at least one way of solving this problem by cracking the "code" in "vineyard."

Likewise, the poem that begins in 2:8 describes the woman's lover as leaping over mountains and hills "like a gazelle." That is an athletic account of a woman's lover, under the simile of a gazelle, but it is not any ordinary way of describing. Gazelles might have been very vigorous and graceful—as might a woman's lover—but we don't really know more than that about connotations the ancient Hebrews had in their minds about gazelles, except that they were swift. Did they think of them as graceful? Did they consider their color to be important? We simply do not know.

I want to identify both the foxes and the gazelles as codes: words, images, metaphors that the writers, singers, and hearers in that culture knew much about, seeing them in their familiar surroundings often, hearing stories about them from their fathers and their grandmothers. Which is to say, they could "decode" the terms and references to the cloud of connotations surrounding them. The foxes and gazelles could contribute meaning to their poetry without their having to spell it out. I refer to them as "codes" because the text does not explain them, and the original hearers and readers did not need them to be explained. But we do not participate in the complexes of meaning and connotation that lie behind the poems.

I do not propose that the people reciting, singing, or hearing the Song of Songs thought that the gazelles and deer concealed anything. They are not cyphers of the sorts that modern militaries characteristically use in their coded messages, especially the ones that might be intercepted by others than their friends. That is our ordinary, modern sense of a "code": something that will go only to someone prepared and permitted to see through it to its meaning but that will not be understood by anyone not in possession of the meanings of the code words. I do not mean the code in that way. I use it to describe words, ideas, situations that may be opaque to us, but not to "them," whoever "they" may be. Not that the codes are secrets, but simply that those who used them to say what they wished to say knew what they meant by them, and they supposed that anyone who read or heard would also know. The Hebrew Bible, including the Song of Songs, was written not for us but for Hebrew-speaking Israelites a long time ago. The fact that sometimes we do not know what they meant is not because we are their enemies, but simply that they had knowledge from their culture that we do not share, and that they did not need to share explicitly with themselves, because they already had it.

For instance, the male lover is sometimes said to "graze among the lilies" in the woman's garden. That a human would "graze" is itself a somewhat odd way to say anything, and we may assume that the idea is a metaphor. Of what it is a metaphor is at best difficult to figure out. I can only guess that it refers to some kind of sexual activity, but they don't tell us either that it is that or what kind it is. Nor do they interpret the "lilies" to us. I suspect that "grazing among the lilies" is a metaphorical code for some way or occasion of making love, but there is no possibility of proving that or of describing it.

I am fascinated by the ways in which the love poetry of the Song of Songs passes us by because of its codes, and I hope that I may help to "decode" some of the words and ideas, of which they knew and understood the meanings, but we do not. I do not promise that I am able to do so. That doesn't trouble me, as I think some mysteries in what we read are helpful to keep us interested. I will note what seem to me "codes" as we go along. And readers may very well perceive some codes that I don't recognize. That does not trouble me either. I am most interested that my readers' vigorously use their own minds and imaginations.

Translating Hebrew

Translating ancient Hebrew to English poses some special problems. The gender distinctions of pronouns, already mentioned, is one of them, which English does not share. In such cases, we need to specify a gender if we can, and sometimes we must use an explanatory note.

Translating Hebrew verbal forms meets some particular problems. The central issue is the verbal tenses. Hebrew has two tenses, called by grammarians "perfect" and "imperfect." The perfect form is defined by affixes, ordinarily of pronouns, and the imperfect is defined by both prefixes and some affixes. The problem is that classical Hebrew tenses were what grammarians call "aspectual" and do not involve necessary time reference, as English tenses do. The main thing that English tenses tell us in their many forms is *when* an action takes place: "I am going" (now); "I go" (sometimes); "I will go;" "I went (some time ago);" "I have gone;" "I had gone (before something else);" "I will have gone (before I do that);" etc. I emphasize that such references to the time of the action are not present in classical Hebrew (modern Hebrew has added them). Therefore, when you translate a Hebrew verb into English, you instantly distort its meaning. The English verb contains meanings that the Hebrew verb does not.

The aspectual Hebrew perfect tense refers to action grasped as complete, which often, but not always, means "past." The imperfect presents action in process, not completed, which often, but not always, means "present" or "future." To complicate the problem, there are places where particular forms reverse these tense meanings—mostly they happen in narrative. But the forms do not include the time of the action. Only the context tells us that, and it is often ambiguous.

I illustrate the problem from the beginning of Song, chapter 3. Verse 1 has four verb forms, all four of them the perfect tense

OVERTURE

in Hebrew, the tense of action seen as complete. I translate them as follows:

> On my bed in the night   I sought the one I love,
>   sought him, but didn't find him.

The second and third lines have two verb forms each, and three of them I have translated as past and one as present ("love"). It would be possible to translate all four as present, as generalized actions, but the poem seems to be speaking of a particular night's experiences. Hence I translated all but one verb as past. It would have been ridiculous to translate "the one I love" as "the one I loved." (Small side remark: "I" is not the Hebrew pronoun but is "my self," *naphšiy*.) But "love" is a general statement, not confined to the particular moment.

V. 2 continues differently. In the four lines are six verb forms:

So I get up and go around the city,   around streets and squares.
    I seek the one I love,   sought him but didn't find him.

In the first line, the two verbs are both imperfects, which I have translated as present. The third line has one imperfect ("seek") and the same perfect ("love") as in v. 1. But the fourth line is the same as in the prior verse, with two perfects ("sought" and "didn't find"). I would argue that the first three forms ("get up," "go," "seek") have to do with action grasped as incomplete, action in process. But the process ends in the last line, and therefore the perfect forms are the right ones: "sought" and "didn't find." Now, perhaps this is being too literal in translating. As Hebrew verbs do not have necessary time reference, it's sometimes quite legitimate to use the English past, as in v. 2: "got up," "went," "sought," or "searched for." If I did that, I think it necessary to include a note that explains what I have done. There are some further instances in the same poem, but I think this is enough to make the point.

I intend to translate into idiomatic English in a style not terribly casual and not strictly literal but, I deeply hope, not stiff. I have made no real effort to write poetry of my own. I asked Anita Sullivan, my wife and a published poet, for assistance in this. Though she is innocent of all Hebrew, she is an expert reader and a gracious editor, and I absolve her of all responsibility for any of it, with immense gratitude for help. Most scholarly translations make no pretense of presenting English poetry (or poetry in any other language). The most successful effort to render the book in English poetry in my opinion is that of Marcia Falk, *Love Lyrics from the Bible: The Song of Songs: A New Translation and Interpretation* (see Bibliography), a revised English Department Ph.D. dissertation at Stanford University, of which I was privileged to be one of the advisors. Dr. Falk is a very talented poet.

Interpretive Essays

The essays on the individual poems are intended to help readers to understand two basic matters: first, how I perceive the poems working as poems, explaining poetic structures and how they are used and the words they are used for. I will look into line structures, figures of speech, specific cultural backgrounds of phrases, concepts, relationships where they can be understood, and the implications and connotations of words, phrases, and expressions in Hebrew. Second, I want to discuss how the poems present and understand love in their own ways, hoping that readers will keep in mind that the Song of Songs is an old Hebrew book, and as such is different from a modern English one.

However, the book itself makes me think that human love has changed little over the millennia, no matter how languages, customs, and ceremonies have changed. Human beings remain human beings, no matter what their languages, cultures, histories, and assumptions about life. Those latter factors assumed by the Song of Songs are different from the same factors in the lives of readers of this book—of whom I am one. It may very well be that my understanding of the love that these poems contain will be different from what other readers see in it. Though I hope that you will take my views of the texts seriously, I cannot require you to agree with those views, and I encourage you to read and understand with your own minds.

It should be quite easy to keep in mind that the book represents its characters as young and as single. Though marriage is mentioned, it seems not to apply to any of the characters except to Solomon (3:11) and to a couple of mothers.

This may be the place to notice that the Song of Songs is traditionally publicly read by Jews at the ceremony of Passover, the springtime festival commemorating the Israelite Exodus from Egypt under the leadership of Moses. That the Song is read on that ceremonial occasion acknowledges that the Passover festival is also in every traditional sense a celebration of Spring and all that it stands for.

This Book's Arrangement

The presentation of what follows is basically simple. First comes the Hebrew text of each poem, in Hebrew letters. I have reproduced the Hebrew script with the characters for vowels and accents, because the text appears that way in modern printed Bibles. To be sure, the vowel signs were added centuries later, in the Middle Ages. Surely the language contained vowels before then, but they were not given written form.

My translation into English follows the Hebrew text, after which come some numbered notes about certain relatively technical problems in the text, followed by the essay of literary interpretation of each poem. After all of the translated and commented poems comes an "Afterword," written at my invitation by Anita Sullivan, my wife and a poet. Her perceptions as a modern poet of the old Hebrew poems, as I have translated them, takes some different directions from mine, which I find both interesting and helpful for readers. Having close access at home with someone intimate with modern poetry seemed to me to propose the value of another voice, and I am most grateful to Anita for this Afterword. At the very end of the book is a bibliography of works that I have used.

2

The Song of Songs

CH. 1:1

שיר השירים אשר לשלמה

The song of the songs that are (or is)
to (or for or by) Solomon

Commentary

This line is presented in the printed biblical text as chapter 1, v. 1, but it is actually the Hebrew title of the book. Most books do not have their titles as their first lines. Many English Bibles title the book "Song of Solomon." I will show later why I do not accept that title.

The Hebrew is remarkably alliterative and musical: four words, five uses of the letter š, pronounced "sh," all told five different consonants, six different vowels. I consider that a very condensed expression. The vowels were added to the Hebrew text many centuries later. Languages change constantly, and this one had perhaps up to thirteen hundred years to change. I will return to this matter.

The question is what the title means. Literally, it says, "The song of the songs that are [or is] to [or for] Solomon." "The song of the songs" is a distinctively Hebrew phrase, called in the grammars a "construct" relation, formed in the same way that, for instance, "the house of the man" is formed, a possessive phrase which could as well be translated "the man's house." But "the songs' song" seems not an immediately sensible English way of saying anything.

The Hebrew Bible has other phrases built like this one: for example "holy of the holies" (q^edoš haqqedošiym, Exod 26:33), "servant of servants" (*'ebed ⁽ᵃ⁾badiym*, Gen 9:25), perhaps "slave of slaves," "king of kings" (*melek melakiym*, Ezek 26:7)—only the first of these three has the definite article on the plural noun which "The song of the songs" has. In each case, the phrase seems to refer to the most important instance in its category, the "most holy place," a "most abject slave," a "most exalted king." "The song of the songs" in our title is taken by some scholars, therefore, as a superlative, something like "the finest of the songs." It should be added that *šiyr*, "song," may also mean "poem," not necessarily sung, though perhaps received mainly by hearing.

I remain slightly uncertain of the superlative meaning of this phrase, but I will not deny it. I also want to imitate the alliteration in the Hebrew perhaps, with something like "The finest songs Solomon sang"—not quite the right alliterative consonant, and freely adding the idea of "sang" into it for the purpose of alliteration. Several scholars have taken the singular "song" in the title to mean that the book is a single poem, not a collection or anthology. I hold the view of an anthology, and I have looked at that issue in the Overture and will look further in the individual essays.

The relative phrase in "the song of the songs that are (or is) Solomon's" is ambiguous in Hebrew: "that" has no indication of number. Should we think "the song that is" or "the songs that are" Solomon's? There is no decisive answer. "The finest songs" intends to be inconclusive but leans toward the plural sense. I could have said "the finest of the songs." The phrase that I have translated "that are Solomon's," has several possibilities. We have the preposition *le*, which can mean "belonging to," "having to do with," or even "by." Of those three meanings, I am willing to consider the first two, preferring the second, but, as will appear almost immediately, I cannot accept the third.

CH. 1:2–4

ישקני מנשיקות פיהו
כי-טובים דודיך מיין לריח שמניך טובים
שמן תורק שמך על-כן עלמות אהבוך
משכני אחריך נרוצה הביאני המלך חדריו
נגילה ונשמחה בך נזכירה דדיך מיין
מישרים אהבוך

{she}

He kisses me[a]—delicious kisses.

Your loving, better than wine	³ or your fragrant oils,
your very name, poured oil,	for all that, girls[b] love you.
⁴ Draw me along, let's run—	the king leads me to his rooms—
joyous and happy,	we celebrate your loving, better than wine;
	they're right[c] to love you.

The Song of Songs

Notes on the translation

a. Many translators render this verb as a kind of subjunctive: "Let him kiss me" or "May he kiss me." I explain below why I do not. This line is put in italic print in order to suggest that the sentence is thought in someone's head but not stated out loud.

b. I use "girls" to translate ʿ*alamowt*, which signifies not little girls but young women of marriageable age 13 and is not the same as *našiym*, the usual word for "women." Some think "girls" demeaning, but in this case, I think it is simply accurate, and I do not intend to demean persons of any gender or any age.

c. *The Concise Dictionary of Classical Hebrew*, ed. David J. Clines (Sheffield: Sheffield Phoenix, 2009, *s.v.* מישרים) gives *meyšariym*, "right," as meaning a kind of wine, perhaps misspelled from *meyraš*, "new wine." That is a nice parallel to the words just before, loving him more than wine, but I don't want to reverse the letters. Perhaps it's a pun. Hebrew poets and other writers loved puns. The problem, however, is that *meyšariym* is a masculine plural nominal form. It might be best to take the word as an abstract, something like "it's right that they love you."

Commentary

The first line of this very brief poem is a single line without a parallel. It might almost be considered as a motto for the entire book. Beginning with the King James Version in 1611, the translation mentioned in note a, above, "let him kiss me" has often been used both in translations of the Bible into English and in books, scholarly or not. I think that the form of the verb allows but does not require that meaning. It would turn the line at least, if not the rest of the poem, into a wishful approach to loving. I see nothing wishful about the rest of this poem, which seems to me to portray remembered acts of loving. "Your loving, better than wine" is not a hypothetical statement, but if it looks forward it does so on the basis of past experience.

There is also a structural reason for the first line to be by itself. The entire short poem has ten lines, the first five being description, the second five action. The opening five-line section is in the order 3 + 2, the first lines as a tercet. The second section is in the order 2 + 3, the last three lines forming the tercet. That kind of mirror structure occurs more than once in the book, and such ways of putting ideas together as well as of distinguishing them are important for poetry. Such a structure is emphasized by the words "loving, better than wine" in both the second line (v. 2b) and the next-to-last line (v. 4d). It is structurally matched by the girls' "loving" in the last lines of both stanzas. The symmetrical placement must be intentional. It is a deliberate combination of free-wheeling love and closely structured poetry. That should not be a surprise. In any language the most well-formed poetry sometimes presents the freest activities.

Another aspect of the first line is that its third-person verb is supplanted in the rest of the poem by second-person addresses, a device that occurs quite often in the poems. "He" becomes "you," and that masculine "you" shows that "she" is the speaker. Except for "I" and "we," Hebrew pronouns have genders, unlike English, which has gender only in "he" and "she."

In the first line, the two kissing words make it clear that kissing is the point of the line, and the two words are long, a verb and cognate noun, very strong, and right together, as the transliteration shows: *yiššaqeni minnešiyqowt*, "He kisses me with kisses." My translation of what follows is not literal: the Hebrew says "kisses of his mouth," and "delicious" stands for "of his mouth." Some scholars have argued that "mouth" is there to distinguish the kissing from nose kisses. A few cultures have practiced such kissing, but ancient Israel did not. The Hebrew Bible makes no mention of nose kisses, and the suggestion that "mouth" distinguishes the kisses from other kinds seems to me pedantic. In the absence of any kissing being ruled out, the mention of "his mouth" seems in fact a bit lame. Does she want to say that she very much enjoys his kissing? I concluded to translate interpretively, "delicious kisses."

There is a certain pleasure in suggesting that this first line of the first poem presents us with what I wish to call a "code." This kissing had meanings to the poets and hearers of these poems that escape us, simply because we belong to a culture that has its own ideas about kissing, just as the ancient Hebrews had their own ideas about it. Our problem is that we don't really know what their ideas were, though we do know what ours are. We have several well-known words that suggest several different kinds of "mouth-kisses," such as "peck," "smooch," and "tongue" kissing. I have seen nothing corresponding to such different kinds of kissing in the Hebrew Bible. So we can only guess at what the Hebrew culture thought about kissing. My guess in this poem is that the female speaker of the poem really liked her fellow's kissing, and that is why I have substituted "delicious" for the words "of his mouth." The latter phrase seems to me, in fact, rather boringly obvious. But "delicious" also contains the reference to the mouth's kissing. And remember that by code I do not mean something that the poem is trying to hide. It is simply that they knew in their context what they meant, and we do not. So we must guess. We will be guessing often in the poems that follow.

An additional idea came my way. The people in this book, with few exceptions, are quite young. Exceptions are Solomon, soldiers, some police guards, and various mothers. Girls in Israel and other ancient cultures often married soon after embarking on menstruation. Is our "she" much older than thirteen? We cannot know. But the thought came: do you remember your first kiss? Not just the very first one after your parents and aunts and uncles, but the first actual sexual kiss? I confess that I don't recall mine, which was a very long time ago, but it was at the time very important. The kissing in this poem may be thought of in that way, a continuation of that memorable first one, when "his" (or "her") mouth first really met yours, and nothing was ever the same again. So the "delicious kisses" propose something forthright and vigorous and entailing the mouths the Hebrew specifies.

The central image of the rest of the poem is the combination of oil and wine. The oils are cooking oils, such as olive oil, or cosmetic oils for sunburn or deodorants, which both men and women evidently used to make themselves sexually more attractive. In that hot climate, bodily odors would have been sometimes quite overpowering. The remarkable term "poured oil" for his name (I have freely added "very" to "name" in order to be emphatic) must propose a sexy quality to the name, perhaps even to its pronunciation. To be sure, neither his name nor hers is ever pronounced in the book. The oils therefore are one of the reasons the "girls love you," and the lover's "loving" is better than wine, "better" being a way of saying "more pleasing." "Loving," both here and in the next-to-last line, plural in Hebrew (*dowdiym*), refers, I think, not to love in the abstract—a different word, *'ahabah*, frequently used in the *Song*—but to multiple acts of making love, not necessarily to the point of intercourse. Wine in this poem decidedly comes out second best to making love, though surely a way of enhancing the experience. At the same time, there is no thought that wine lacks pleasures, as the rest of the book makes clear. Palestine was very good wine country.

With "girls love you," we are back in the realm of the abstract, for this verb is not *dowd*, as in vv. 2 and 3, but the more abstract *'hb*, closer to "being in love" than to the "acts of loving" that *dowdiym* signifies. Later we will see that *dowd* is also the usual word the woman uses for her lover. So the "loving" and the "lover" are the same word, or at least the same sound. But as we will see, the plural is always used to mean the loving, and she never admits to plural lovers.

Again in v. 4 is a shift between second to third person. "Draw me along, let's run" is addressed to the man, and she refers to him in a frequent metaphor for a lover as "the king," the owner of the rooms to which they run. This might have been another excuse to think of Solomon as the author. In a culture as small as Israel, lovers could quite easily think of each other as "kings" and "queens," who would have been familiar persons, however powerful. In this case "king" is honorifically metaphorical—and we may be sure that in calling him "the king" she thinks of herself as "the queen." The image of bringing a lover to rooms or a house is quite common in the Song. It occurs three other times: he does the bringing in 2:4, and she brings him to her mother's house in 3:4 and 8:2, surely a highly symbolic place.

Describing celebration or his loving as better than wine is a double meaning I incline to accept. Whether celebration or loving, it produces joy and happiness, interestingly, for a plural "we." As the woman is the speaker in this poem, the "we" is most likely the "girls" who love him in v. 3 and again in v. 4. She had not mentioned the girls as coming with her to the king's rooms. But here are plural people being happy and celebrating him ("you," v. 4d, is masculine singular), and she is not jealous of their presence. On the contrary, "they are right" to love him. Exum takes the plural people and girls as images of the courtesans in the king's harem.[1] The echo of "girls love you" (v. 3) would lend further credence to the fantasy of a king's "rooms," in which the presence of other women might be expected. And the closing line, "they are right to love you," brings back the girls of v. 3c, adding the parallel to their loving him in the last lines of the two five-line stanzas as well as the implied pun in "right," *mešariym* (see note c, above), to the wine that was earlier praised. It is a satisfying conclusion to a tightly organized short poem.

---

1. Good, *Irony in the Old Testament* (2nd ed.), 182.

CH. 1:5–6

שחורה אני ונאוה בנות ירושלם
כאהלי קדר כיריעות שלמה
אל-תראוני שאני שחרחרת ששזפתני השמש
בני אמי נחרו-בי שמני נטרה את-הכרמים
כרמי שלי לא נטרתי

                    {she}

5 Black I am and beautiful,   Jerusalem's daughters,
        like Qedar's tents,   Solomon's curtains.
6 Don't stare at me, blackened   The sun caught sight of me.
        as I am.
My mother's sons snorted[a] at me,   sent me to secure the vineyards.
        My very own vineyard I've not secured.

The Song of Songs

Notes on the Translation

a. "Snorted" is a verb that usually describes the sounds horses make, and it suggests brothers ordering little sisters around.

Commentary

"Black" signifies sunburn here, not genetically black skin as in Africa. Nevertheless, many earlier translations seem to have thought of African-style blackness in translating, "Black am I, but beautiful." As victims of cultural backgrounds, we are sometimes caught by the false imagination that beauty seldom accompanies black skin. But the Hebrew conjunction, which sometimes suggests "but," is usually the simpler "and." It is interesting to find a woman in the Hebrew Bible who defends and describes her own beauty. There is no fear of pride, it seems.

The blackness is explained in v. 6, where I have used "blackened" for a form of *šeḥowrah* intensified by a repeated syllable, *šeḥarḥoret*. There it is explained by sunburn. "Like Qedar's tents," in the second couplet of v. 5, is a comparison of her hair to tents made of black goat's hair, and to "Solomon's curtains." Wherever the latter might have been and however decorated, they might be the same material. But the black of goats' hair is, in effect, "blacker" than the black of sunburn, and in 4:1, he compares her hair specifically to goats' hair.

The first couplet of v. 6 shows an alliterative style quite common in Hebrew, piling up uses of the consonant we suppose sounded as "sh." Two š's in the first line, four in the second. Sound matters in poetry, and these š's may sound mildly irritated.

In the last tercet of v. 6, we learn that she got her sunburn when she was sent by overbearing brothers out to guard the vineyards in the day's heat. The image that shows the brothers acting like, well, older brothers is the verb *naḥar*, which usually describes the snorting of horses. I like that image much better than, for instance, NJPS's "quarreled." There is no quarreling about it, only commanding, being imperious. Exum is better: "were angry with me"; but it is still too general to be vivid. We should also notice an echo, perhaps even a sound-play, in the sound of *naḥar*, "snort," to "black," *šehḥorah*. Both words have a "*ḥ*" and an "*r*" in the same order. Surely deliberate, perhaps a pun. But what we might take as an English sound-play between "sun" and "sons" is not one in Hebrew.

Then we meet a new metaphor: the vineyard. She is sent out to "secure" the vineyards, which entails not only weeding and watching growth but also protecting them against birds, foxes (see 2:15), and perhaps human plunderers. Well, she has done it, but there is that other vineyard, her very own, for which she found excuses not to "secure." Her phrase is telling: she could have said just "my vineyard," (*karmiy*), but she says *karmiy šelliy*, "my vineyard that's (all?) mine." I wonder whether to leave the reader to infer what "my vineyard" means, or whether to state the obvious. I will satisfy myself by referring to 2:15 again and also to 8:12, where the same phrase defines a man's own vineyard. If it is still not clear, ask your mother. The poets preferred to leave the metaphorical understanding to us, and that too demonstrates sophistication.

CH. 1:7–8

הגידה לי שאהבה נפשי איכה תרעה
איכה תרביץ בצהרים
שלמה אהיה כעטיה על עדרי חבריך
אם-לא תדעי לך היפה בנשים
צאי-לך בעקבי הצאן ורעי את-גדיתיך
על משכנות הרעים

{she}

⁷ Tell me, my life's love,   where you pasture,
            where you rest at noon?
Why should I be covered   beside your friends' flocks?

{he}

⁸ If you don't know,   most beautiful woman,[a]
follow the sheep tracks   and pasture your kids
       by the shepherds' tents.

The Song of Songs

Notes on the translation

a. The Hebrew actually says "most beautiful of women," using the plural *našiym*. I slightly prefer the shorter equivalent. "Most beautiful" is adequate to the point.

Commentary

In this dialogue poem, she asks a question in the first five line stanza, and he answers it (in some sense) in the second. Like the first poem, this one has two stanzas of five lines, and like the other poem, they are structured in an opposite order, 3 + 2 followed by 2 + 3. That opposition satisfyingly distinguishes the two speakers, but makes them also alike in the lengths of their two parts. The opposition is even more subtly done. In the woman's opening tercet, the second and third lines are in a synonymous parallelism and the following couplet is not parallel. The man's stanza has the opposite structure: it starts with a non-parallel couplet and follows with a tercet of which the first two lines are in parallel. This carefully interlocked structure is another piece of evidence that, though this may be folk-poetry, it is poetically sophisticated. Such a structure would also be an aid to memory, if the poem was being recited or sung.

There is more to this careful structure. She uses the verb *r'h*, "to pasture," in her second line, v. 7b. He uses the same verb in his fourth line, v. 8d. These verbal repetitions are in the opposite places, the second line and the next to last of the ten lines. Again, she uses the preposition *'al* ("by, beside") in her last line, and he uses the same preposition in his last line. Such carefully placed repetitions are not accidental. They may, of course, have come about in the process of revisions, in oral or written form. There is no way to know. But they demonstrate the presence of art.

We are out in the country, where both lovers herd small animals. His are sheep, as he is among the shepherds and mentions "sheep tracks" as clues to his whereabouts, where hers are goats. Was it common practice in Israel that men herded sheep, and women herded goats? I know of no reason to think so—or to think not. She wishes to spend part of the day with him, bringing their flocks together. And she wants his friends to be elsewhere so that they can be free to make love. If the friends were to be present, she would have to be properly dressed, "covered up."

He proposes to be near the camp ground ("beside the shepherds' tents"), indicating that his friends, the shepherds, will not be there. The animals can take care of themselves for the time being. So the implied love-making is viewed in the poem as a future possibility, to be wished. We may well hope in ourselves that it happened.

CH. 1:9—2:3

לסוסתי ברכבי פרעה דמיתיך רעיתי
נאוו לחייך בתרים צוארך בחרוזים
תורי זהב נעשה-לך עם נקדות הכסף
עד-שהמלך במסבו נרדי נתן ריחו
צרור המר דודי לי בין שדי ילין
אשכל הכפר דודי לי בכרמי עין-גדי
הנך יפה רעיתי הנך יפה
עיניך יונים
הנך יפה דודי אף נעים
אף-ערשנו רעננה
קרות בתינו ארזים רחיטנו ברותים
אני חבצלת חשרון שושנת העמקים
כשושנה בין החוחים כן רעיתי בין הבנות
כתפוח בעצי היער כן דודי בין הבנים
בצלו חמדתי וישבתי ופריו מתוק לחכי

The Song of Songs

{he}

⁹ I compare you, my love,   to a mare among Pharaoh's chariots.

¹⁰ Your cheeks are lovely with pendants,   your neck with jewels.

¹¹ We'll make you golden pendants   with silver beads.

{she}

¹² While the king is in his couch   my nard gives out its fragrance.

¹³ A bundle of myrrh, my lover,ᵃ   lying between my breasts;

¹⁴ A henna cluster, my lover,   like En-Gedi's vineyards.

{he}

¹⁵ Oh, you are beautiful, love;   Oh, beautiful, your eyes doves.

{she}

¹⁶ Oh, you are beautiful, lover,   better yet, delightful; still better, our bed is luxuriant.

¹⁷ Our house's beams are cedar,   the rafters juniper.

2:¹ I am a rose in Sharon,ᵇ   a lily from the valleyᶜ

{he}

² Like a lily among thistles,   my love among daughters.

{she}

³ Like an apple in the forest,   my lover among sons.

I delight to sit in his shade,   and his fruit is sweet on my palate.

THE SONG OF SONGS

Notes on the Translation

a. I have reversed the order of the two lines from the Hebrew, preferring this for the translation.

b. This flower is not the one known in North America as the "rose of Sharon." Therefore I have substituted the preposition "in." Some scholars think that "rose" is actually a crocus. I choose "rose" for euphony.

c. Likewise, this flower is not the one known in North America as "lily of the valley." It is an ordinary lily that sometimes grows in valleys, and I have again changed the preposition. Clearly these North American flowers were named on the supposition that our passage referred to them.

Commentary

Here is another dialogue, in which the lovers speak back and forth to each other. The setting is in the countryside, if 1:16–17 is any indication. On the other hand, 1:12 might suggest a bedroom, but I take "couch" as a metaphor for wherever he lies down. 2:1–3 might seem a separate poem, but I prefer to see it as the continuation of the preceding part.

His opening simile is an odd one in some ways. Verses 9–11 surely propose that Pharaoh's chariot-horses were very beautifully decorated. But Marvin Pope found the description of a military trick used against an Egyptian invasion of Western Asia in the early 1400s, BCE,[1] that described the enemies' ruse of sending a mare among the Egyptians' chariots as a way to distract the chariot stallions from their duties, as the mare was carefully chosen to be in heat. This is a delightfully imaginative and inventive interpretation, which even Robert Alter accepts.[2] I wish I could do the same, but nothing in the rest of the poem remotely suggests that disruption is any part of what is going on. Rather, the simile

1. Exum, *Song of Songs*, 95.
2. Alter, *The Art of Biblical Poetry*, 193.

runs to the woman's beauty, set off by jewelry on her head and neck. Exum suggests sensibly that, as horses are either stallions or mares, and the poet was describing a woman, she could not very well be called a stallion, so the poet properly referred to her as a beautifully decorated mare. Israelite poets doubtless supposed, as did everyone else at the time, that Egyptian royal chariots were the most impressively beautiful chariots imaginable. It seems unlikely that they knew anything about the details of fitting them or their horses out some centuries before.

The "pendants" may be earrings, though they might have hung from the hair. Who the "we" are, who promise to make gold and silver pendants, is not evident. The man seems to count himself among "companions" to make the fine jewelry for a beautiful woman. The book refers often to jewelry, perhaps allusions to wished-for wealth in addition to feminine beauty. She echoes the mention of Pharaoh by referring to her lover as the king on his couch. We do not know whether the couch is in the king's "rooms" as in 1:4. "King" is surely, however, the same metaphor as in that passage, and the "couch" may simply mean wherever the lovers lie down.

These poems frequently refer to spices, perfumes, and good smells. She wears "nard," a very fragrant spice, the full name of which is spikenard, and describes her lover as a bundle of myrrh lying between her breasts. He is also a cluster of henna blossoms, said to have a strong scent like roses. These exotic smells (myrrh, after all, had to be brought to Israel from Arabia or India by caravan, Gen 37:25) propose rather specific flavors, well known to the ancient hearers and readers as sexually suggestive. En-Gedi (the "spring of the kid") on the shore of the Dead Sea is said to have been known as an ancient location of the production of perfumes, and the name of the place also reminds us of the kids that she herds in 1:8. This tangle of allusions and references adds up to a complex and subtle sense of the lovers' physical properties and their perceptions of them.

The following two stanzas are a pair, each lover describing the other's beauty. His stanza seems somewhat under-emphatic. "Your eyes [are] doves" may strike us as a rather lame lover's description.

It is doubtless a code, the precise meaning of which is not immediately available to us. She is described in the metaphor of a dove in 2:14, but that is herself, not only her eyes. We may think of the soft grey of doves, but we do not know if the color of her eyes was the poet's point. We might also think of doves' presumed softness, but likewise we do not know whether the ancient Hebrews thought of them in that way. We need to keep in our minds that these love poems are very old and totally Hebrew. There was a time when they were new. In the meantime, the Bible has become a very familiar book, often copied and quoted. Any contemporary woman who wishes to warn her lover away from calling her eyes doves can freely do so, and he would be wise to take the warning. But the book uses the image quite frequently, and the ancient poets must have the right to use their own images. We can use our imaginations to realize that these images, more than 2,000 years old, give us both entry into and blockage from the ancient mind.

We should not be surprised that a woman might use the same adjective (in masculine form) for her lover that he used for her: "beautiful." She adds other adjectives: "delightful" and, for the bed, "luxuriant." We discover in v. 17 that the bed is out in the wild, where the cedar boughs and the junipers take the place of beams and rafters.

In 2:1, she changes the subject to describe herself as two different kinds of flowers. I explained in the notes that "rose of Sharon" and "lily of the valleys" do not mean the flowers so named and familiar to us in North America, but that "Sharon" and "the valleys" are the locations where the roses (or crocuses) and lilies were to be found. The seemingly familiar flower names show another instance of how biblical phrases have become familiar English ones.

The male lover echoes the "lily," but compares it favorably to thistles that may surround it, and that too should make us notice that she did not call herself the kind of flower we would think of as a "lily of the valley." As is so frequent in this book, groups of women are referred to as "daughters." Perhaps we need to notice too that the beloved woman is compared to a lily among thistles, the latter being the metaphor for the daughters, and perhaps the "daughters" would not appreciate it.

She echoes him in a similar metaphor, calling men in general "sons" and comparing him to an apple among the forest trees, surely, as the following line shows, meaning not only the fruit but also the tree. The tree gives shade, welcome in that sometimes torrid climate, and a fresh apple (or apricot, as some scholars identify the fruit) helps to offset the discomfort of the hot sun.

We may also notice that the reference in the last stanza to the apple is a possible linking word. a mnemonic device for the reciter or singer of the next poem, which in v. 5 refers again to apples.

CH. 2:4–7

הביאני אל-בית היין ודגלו עלי אהבה
סמכוני באשישות רפדוני בתפוחים
כי-חולת אהבה אני
שמאלו תחת לראשי וימינו תחבקני
השבעתי אתכם בנות ירושלם בצבאות או באילות השדה
אם-תעירו ואם-תעוררו את-האהבה עד שתחפץ

{she}

⁴ He brings me to the house of wine,   and glances[a] love upon me.

⁵ Revive me with raisin cakes,   spread out apples for me,
for I'm faint with love.

⁶ His left hand under my head,   his right hand caresses me.

⁷ I put you on oath, Jerusalem's daughters,   by the gazelles or the does[b] of wild,
don't rouse or awaken   love until it wishes.

Notes on the Translation

a. The word is a noun meaning also something like "banner." Further comment below.
b. The word refers to female deer.

Commentary

The action of this short poem seems to occur first in "the house of wine" and second in bed somewhere unspecified. The latter location seems to be private enough for the man's earlier "glance" to be easily interpreted.

Exum prefers "banner" to "glance" for a noun that can mean either.[1] The banner seems to me an intrusive image here, suggesting something military, or at least the kind of public place that has not been suggested. If "banner" had some sexual connotation, I would like it better. It seems that wine-drinking and eating take place in one space, sleeping and allied activities in another.

Exactly what a "house of wine" means is not certain. A bar? A restaurant, or its equivalent in ancient Israel? A brothel? A private hideaway? Exum chooses the last option, thinking of a private house combined with the private drinking of wine.[2] She thinks it is not in any sense a public place. Clearly one did not only drink there. The food might be intended to encourage love-making: raisin cakes derived, of course, from grapes, but also apples, to which she compares her lover in 2:3. Whether the "apples," *tappuwḥiym*, were apricots, we cannot know certainly; apricots might have been considered sexy as apples were, and these fruits may have been considered aphrodisiacs. Surely they were not thought to decrease desire. She is already "faint (or weak) with love," and no one in that condition would look to impede desire. The verb "spread out" is a very rare one, used elsewhere only in Job 17:13 and 41:22. In the former verse, it has to do with "spreading out" a bed, but how that

1. Exum, *Song of Songs*, 115.
2. Ibid., 114–15.

spreading is like the kind you would do with apples (or apricots) is not clear. The "apples," moreover, having appeared at the end of the foregoing poem, is doubtless also a linking word in the oral collecting of the poems.

"Revive" and "spread out" are masculine plural imperatives. Does she address companions of the lover? Exum notes that masculine verbal forms are used elsewhere for female addressees, as close by as "rouse" and "awaken" in v. 7d (*ta'owruw, ta'owr^{e}ruw*).[3] But she proposes another possibility that I like better: the address is to the audience, which, at least in thought, is thus brought into the scene.[4] And that idea suggests again the situation of reciting or singing the poem.

At v. 6 we are at a place where there is privacy of the sort that allows making love. No hint is given whether it is somewhere in the countryside or is in a room. The expression is very compressed, describing only the position of the lover's hands, which is enough to give us a clear picture and does not complicate the scene with its physical setting.

We should understand the oath commanded in v. 7 to "Jerusalem's daughters" as being rhetorical expansion, not anything that is actually said to anyone. Surely those women were not assumed to be in attendance at the love-making. The oath on gazelles and does presents a pair of images very frequent in the book. It is another code. We know what an oath is, but in what sense is it to be sworn by the daughters as "by the gazelles and does of the wild?" Is it similar to our oaths that end "so help me God"? Are they named as guarantors of the oath, or witnesses to it? The preposition "by" means "in, with, by," but exactly what that means in a Hebrew oath is not perfectly certain. The phrase occurs again in 3:5. This oath is repeated word for word in 8:3-4 except for the mention of the gazelles and does. The gazelles appear in the next poem, suggesting that the word might also have been a linking word or mnemonic for the reader or singer.

3. Ibid., 116.
4. Ibid., 118.

There is another point about these gazelles and deer, pointed out by Exum.[5] The Hebrew word for gazelles, a feminine plural, is *ṣebaʾowt*, which is spelled and pronounced in exactly the same way as the word meaning "hosts" in the familiar phrase "Yahweh (or "the Lord") of Hosts" in many places in the Hebrew Bible, e.g. 1 Sam 1:3. "Lord of Hosts" is an epithet for a divinity in charge of an army, sometimes of super-human beings, sometimes of humans. She also points out that the "does of the wild," in Hebrew *'ayᵉlowt hassadeh*, is reminiscent of the look and sound of El Shaddai, one of the names given to the Israelite god. I find the latter suggestion less satisfying than the former, but no Hebrew speaker in the ancient period would have missed the double meaning, "gazelles" and "hosts," and many of them might well have noticed the similarity of "does of the wild" and "El Shaddai." Perhaps these proposals go some distance to explain what putting people under oath "by the gazelles and does of the wild" might mean in terms of the power or importance of the words like those spoken. It reminds us, perhaps, of our occasional use of substitutes for swear words, such as "Heck" for "Hell" or "darn" for "damn."

And we must wonder whether some Hebrew speakers might have reversed the reference to gazelles. When they saw or heard the phrase "Yahweh of hosts," might they think "Yahweh of the gazelles." That would put a very different face on Yahweh, in my opinion—perhaps turning him into a god not of avenging or aggressive "hosts" of stars, angels, or armies, but into a deity watching with pleasure over human love-making. It's not an image typical of Yahweh in the Hebrew Bible, but it might well have functioned as a code beneath the surface, and perhaps the Song is the best place to contemplate it. Additionally, "gazelles" may be a linking word to the next poem.

The concluding couplet is an interesting instance of a non-parallel couplet. The sentence continues across both lines, and the two cognate verbs, "rouse" (*taʾowruw*) and "awaken" (*tᵉʾowrᵉruw*), are in the same line, so that the action forbidden is in the first line and the sequel in the second.

---

5. Ibid., 119.

The Song of Songs

The woman certainly speaks this poem, and it is particularly interesting in that it proposes both a tryst in what may have been a public place ("house of wine") and a subsequent period of lovemaking in private. This woman is prepared to propose making love herself, instead of waiting for the man to invite the occasion. It is followed by the oath to the daughters of Jerusalem not to wake the lovers from their love, which I suggested above is rhetorical, not part of a conversation.

CH. 2:8–14

קול דודי הנה-זה בא
מדלג על-ההרים מקפץ על-הגבעות
דומה דודי לצבי או לעפר האילים
הנה-זה עומד אחר כתלנו
משגיח מן החלנות מציץ מן החרכים

ענה דודי ואמר לי
קומי לך רעיתי יפתי ולכי-לך
כי-הנה הסתו עבר הגשם חלף הלך לו
הנצנים נראו בארץ עת הזמיר הגיע
וקול התור נשמע בארצנו
התאנה חנטה פניה והגפנים סמדר נתנו ריח
קומי לכי רעיתי יפתי ולכי-לך
יונתי בחגוי הסלע בסתר המדרגה
הראיני את-מראיך השמיעיני את-קולך
כי-קולך ערב ומראיך נאוה

The Song of Songs

{she}

⁸ The sound of my lover! There! He's coming!
Leaping over mountains, springing over hills
⁹ likeᵃ a gazelle, my lover, a young deer,
there, standing outside the wall, gazing through the windows,
peering in the lattice.
¹⁰ My lover said to me:ᵇ

{he}

Get you up,ᶜ my love, my beauty, and come away.
¹¹ For, look! The winter is past, the rain is finished and gone.
¹² The land blossoming, it's time to sing,
to hear the turtledove out there.
¹³ The first fig ripens, budding vines give out fragrance.
Get you up,ᶜ my love, my beauty, and come away.
¹⁴ My dove, in the rock's clefts, in secret, in the cliff,
show me your body, let me hear your voice,
for your voice is sweet, and your body beautiful.

Notes on the Translation

a. The Hebrew is more effusive than my "like"; it is rather "I compare my lover to a gazelle." I thought compression was appropriate for the translation.

b. The expression here is a common Hebrew phrase: "My lover answered and said to me." As no question has been asked, I have omitted "answered" from the translation.

c. In both these places, I have taken the Hebrew *quwmiy lak* as more intensive than the rather ordinary "Get up," *quwmiy*.

The Song of Songs

The phrase comes closer to meaning "get up for yourself" or "Get you up."

Commentary

An interesting verbal link between the prior poem and this one may, like the references to "apple" in 2:3 and in v. 5, suggest one of the ways in which poems were placed together in the stage of oral transmission. At the end of 2:7 the oath given to the daughters is sworn on "gazelles" and "does of the wild." And here in v. 9, the young man leaping across the hills is described as a "gazelle" and a "young deer," both words related to those in the prior poem. Of course, both words here are masculine in gender, not the feminine genders of the animals in the oath. He would not in any case be likened to a "doe." But the close proximity of the words could well have served to assist the memory of singers or reciters; mention of gazelles and does at the end of one poem would recall the cognates mentioned early in the next poem. Such linking words are well known in oral cultures as ways of gathering differing works into collections. To be sure, they might have been used also by poets writing longer poems, but if so, it seems to me to suggest that the writer borrowed an oral device. I think first of a poet composing an oral poem. How long would it have been before it was written down? There is no way either to guess or to know. And before it was written down, it would surely have undergone many oral revisions.

The woman's exuberant description of her lover's approach, "leaping over the mountains / springing over the hills," is both endearing and exciting. He's an athlete, this fellow. At the same time, the image of his arrival from some distance strongly suggests that this poem is not a continuation of the prior one, and we cannot identify the "house of wine" with the woman's house. Of course, he is coming to see her, as we find in the subsequent lines, standing outside the wall, looking through the windows and the lattice, waiting patiently—or impatiently—for someone to notice that he's there. At least his impatience does not completely overcome his propriety, though he is "peering in the lattice." It would not do for him to break into her house. And that tells us again that it is not the "house of wine."

At v. 10, I over-ruled a frequent Hebrew idiom: "My lover answered and said to me," to give its entire English equivalent. Hebrew writers did not hesitate to write "answered and said" even if no question or prior remark has been introduced. English speakers expect answers to follow questions, or at least prior statements. We might take this as another implication of the poem's oral quality. What follows is the man's speech, presented as if it were quoted by the woman. I have taken the liberty of noting that he is presented as the speaker.

He invites her to come out of the house into which he is peering and enjoy the arrival of spring with all of its inducements to love-making. He recites the signs of spring: the new growth of plants, attractive fragrances, pleasant sights and bird-songs, all suggesting new and renewed life. It is well to recall again that nowadays the Song of Songs is read at Passover in the spring, and this passage is one of its most evident references to the season. The speaker matches those natural pleasures of sight, smell, and sound with her equivalents, the sights of her beautiful form and the sound of her beautiful voice. No mention of fragrance is there, but we may think of it even if the poet left it out.

"Get you up" and "come away" are repeated to the woman, and the idea is resumed with the pleasures of the hidden places, the "clefts of the rocks" and the "secret places" in the cliffs. He was interested earlier in the poem in the appearances of spring, blossoming and budding, and here he echoes those with the appearances of the places in which he wishes to see her—and no doubt also the secret places that he wishes to see in her. Earlier he was also interested in the sounds of spring, bird songs and specifically the turtledove's song. Here, it is her voice that he wishes to hear. The echoes of sight and sound in the second part of the speech hark back to sight and sound in the first part. To be sure, he is more interested, we may gather, in hearing and seeing her, however interesting are the sights of nature's spring. His last two couplets reverse the orders of "form" and "voice," a very simple but effective poetic device.

CH. 2:15–17

מחבלים כרמים וכרמינו סמדר
דודי לי ואני לו הרעה בשושנים
עד שיפוח היום ונסו הצללים
סב דמה-לך דודי לצבי או לעפר האילים
על-הרי בתר

{she}

¹⁵ Catch^a us the foxes,   the little foxes,
who ruin our vineyards   when they are blooming.
¹⁶ My lover is mine, and I am his,   he grazes among the lilies
¹⁷ until the day breathes,   and the shadows fade.
Turn, love, be like^b the gazelle,   or the young deer
on the mountains' ravines.

Notes on the translation

a. The imperative is masculine plural and its meaning is unclear. Who is being urged to catch foxes for whom? And why? Answers are plentiful, and very few of them go together with anything in the passage. The essay is the best place to ponder these questions, among others.

b. Another instance of the verb "compare" (*dmh*) as in 1:9, as well as another use of the images of the gazelle and young deer.

Commentary

This passage has given interpreters fits. It illustrates again one of the difficulties we moderns encounter with ancient literatures: we often do not know the implications and connotations the ancient authors knew. What do the foxes, normal or little, signify? There are, I think, as many different answers as there are interpreters. I find that I am not really helped by the fact, for example, that Ezek 13:4 calls false prophets foxes. Once again we have a code, the connotations of which ancient hearers and readers knew, but we can only guess at it. One of the things we know about foxes is something that has been observed in Europe and North America, and perhaps our poem tells us that ancient Israel knew it as well: foxes are unusual among wild canines in liking grapes. So it is not surprising to hear that they "ruin the vineyards," though it is disconcerting that they do it not when the vineyards are full of grapes but when they are blooming. Nor do we have a clue as to why the "little foxes" are among the ones to be caught. Some scholars have argued that "little foxes" is playful in tone, and that would be delightful, but how to decide it eludes me.

The one significant clue seems to be the use of the vineyard as an image back in 1:6. There "vineyard" surely stood metaphorically for the woman, and more specifically it suggests her sexuality. So the foxes, little as they may be, may suggest boys who wish to try out their own developing sexuality on the young women, whose early sexuality is suggested by the blooming vineyards. Who is addressed with that imperative masculine plural to "catch us" the foxes. And who are those "little foxes?" Are they real foxes or younger men, who have their minds on sexual experience? Are they adult men who are to do that, either for the pleasures of the women or to remove threats to them? And who is addressed with that imperative masculine plural, "catch us"? More codes. I suspect that the imperative is addressed to male friends of the women, inviting them to intervene to protect their women friends.

It is interesting how often in these poems addresses of speech and identifications of characters change. Verse 15 is addressed to plural males, vv. 16–17b describe a single male's connection to the previous female speaker, and v. 17c-e addresses him. Similar shifts have occurred in earlier poems.

The rest of the poem concerns itself entirely with the woman and the man at the poem's center. There is no doubt about him: he is "mine and I am his," which makes it certain that the poem is in the woman's voice, but also proposes the equality of the lovers on all levels. Neither is the sole "owner." He has, as it were, been caught. Are the little foxes, then, nuisances to be removed from the women, who have their lovers and know them? The foxes threaten to ruin the vineyards and are not to be tolerated. But the known lover "grazes among the lilies," which seems from some of the other poems to be a coded metaphor for activity with loved women's bodies. The vineyard has become a figure of the sexuality at risk from the little foxes but safe with the gazelle and the young deer, the ones welcomed to the house and to the beds of lilies, and we can assume that gazelles and deer might well want to graze on the lilies. To be sure, they would likely graze as happily on the vines.

The references to the time of day are not certain. The first couplet of v. 17, "until the day breathes, and the shadows fade" might mean either evening or morning. "Breathing" might be the end of the often terrible heat of the day or the return of the morning, and the fading "shadows" might mean that the surroundings become less visible in the evening or more visible (light as opposed to shadow) at dawn. Another kind of code. Remember, these poets used codes not as a means of concealment but exactly the opposite, but we do not always possess the knowledge they assumed.

The lover is welcomed also to the "mountain's ravines," to those "clefts of rocks" in the previous poem (2:14), where the lover wished to see her beautiful body. "Ravines" is an extraordinarily suggestive sexual image, and it puts the finishing touch to "my lover is mine, and I am his." We may not have closure on the meanings of all of the images in this poem, but we may be closer than we were.

CH. 3:1–5

על משכבי בלילות בקשתי את שאהבה נפשי
בקשתיו ולא מצאתיו
אקומה נא ואסובבה בעיר בשוקים וברחבות
אבקשה את שאהבה נפשי בקשתיו ולא מצאתיו
מצאוני השמרים הסבבים בעיר
את שאהבה נפשי ראיתם
כמעט שעברתי מהם עד שמצאתי את שאהבה נפשי
אחזתיו ולא ארפנו
עד-שהביאתיו אל-בית אמי ואל-חדר הורתי
השבעתי אתכם בנות ירושלם בצבאות או באילות השדה
אם-תעירו ואם-תעוררו את-האהבה עד שתחפץ

{she}

3:¹ In bed at night   I sought my life's love,
   sought, but didn't find him.

² So I got up to go around   its streets and squares,
   in the city,

   seeking my love;[a]   I sought,[b] but didn't find him.

³ The watchmen found me, who roam around the city.
"My love,ᵃ you've seen him?"ᶜ

⁴ I had scarcely passed them when I found my love;ᵃ
I held him and wouldn't let go until I brought him to my mother's house,
the room where she conceived me.

⁵ I put you on oath, Jerusalem's daughters, by the gazelles or the doesᵈ of the wild,
don't rouse or waken love, until it wishes.

Notes on the Translation

a. She refers four times in the poem to the lover in the exact phrase used here, *še'ahᵃbah napšiy*, more literally "the one my life loves." I prefer not to translate Heb. *nepeš* as "soul," as it is not at all what the Greeks meant by *psyche*, their word translated "soul." It is a kind of life force, but I do not want to repeat "my life's love" four times in a relatively short poem.

b. The Hebrew changes tense here. Verse 1 has verbs in the perfect tense, and I have translated them as past. But the verbs in the first three lines of v. 2 are all imperfects, which I translate with past on the perception that tenses without time reference can in fact be translated with whatever time reference applies in the particular poem. The last line of v. 2 has verbs in the perfect tense, "sought" and "didn't find." Moreover, this last line of v. 2 repeats v. 1c.

c. The sentence does not have an interrogative marker, but I think it must be taken as a question, answered in the next verses.

d. Unfortunately "does," female deer (pronounced "doze") and "does," the present tense of "to do" (pronounced "duz"), are in English spelled the same. Here it is the deer.

Commentary

This is the first of two poems in which the woman searches at night for her lover through Jerusalem, the second being a totally different experience narrated in 5:2—6:3. Seeking for her lover at night in her bed perhaps suggests dreams, which might be the equivalent at night of day-dreams. These day-dreams lead to the night-time excursion in the city, whether or not that is also a dream.

The crucial point seems to be seeking and not finding in v. 2d, which is emphasized by the repetition in v. 2d of v. 1c: "Sought him but didn't find him," is continued in the conclusion of the search by her finding the watchmen. She didn't find him, but they found her (this incident is totally different in the other search poem in 5:2ff). Her question to them (I take it as such, though the sentence has no interrogative mark) evokes no response. But the search has a quick conclusion, as she finds her lover and "holds him." That verb comes very close to "grab," the same one used in 2.15 of "catching" the foxes. "Wouldn't release him" almost suggests a mild struggle. The action is certainly vigorous, but the man is evidently not averse to being taken to a place that she thinks of as safe.

But the place is more than just safe. The house is not only the one where the woman lived in her childhood, but includes the very room in which she was conceived. It is without question an awesomely significant place in terms of sexuality. I think it interesting that she calls the house her "mother's house," not her father's house. This is not information strictly about the ownership of the house, which, insofar as the society would have cared about it, would probably have been the property of her father's family. What is important is what happened there involving the woman herself, and the most important point right now is women's work, conception. We may infer that conception, or what leads to it, is at the top of her mind.

Her final oath sworn to Jerusalem's daughters is identical to the one at the end of 2:7, closing with a non-parallel couplet. Indeed, the couplet could be called an enjambement, for the sentence runs across the poetic line-break. Such a poetic device is unusual in Hebrew poetry but by no means absent.

Another interesting thing, both here and in 2:7, is that the daughters are being required to swear an oath about rousing or awakening "love," the abstraction of what goes on between the lovers. The word "love" has the definite article, which makes it all the more abstract. Some scholars and textual editors would like to put different vowels with the word ha'ah^{a}bah, making it ha^{a}hubah. The feminine passive participle, "the beloved." The feminine form of the word strikes me as meaning that she does not want to be awakened. The idea can be understood in this situation only if she and he have been sleeping, which is certainly a likely reading. If the entire poem is a dream, which I doubted at the outset, then almost any meaning works about waking love. I prefer to remain with the abstraction, "love."

The question is whether the oath is opposed to waking up sleeping lovers or to arousing love at its inception. In both places where it is administered, here and at 2:7, the lovers are in fact together and are presumably sleeping or about to do so. In the earlier poem the prior couplet has to do with amorous gestures, his arm under her head and his hand caressing her. Here they have gone to the conception chamber in her mother's house—and what can that be but the intention to make love? Therefore I incline to interpret the waking-rousing words as pointing to sleeping lovers, not to love not yet realized.

The repeated oath rests again on the gazelles and the "does of the wild." "Wild" is literally "the field," which means either an empty, uncultivated field—hence "wild"—or a cultivated one. I think the poet has the former in mind. The gazelles and does (deer) in both oaths are feminine in gender. And the oath is to the women, "Jerusalem's daughters." Once more, we have codes the precise meanings of which are not certain. What was the symbolic force of the gazelles and deer? It was clearly connected to love, as these animals are males when they are connected to her lover dashing over the mountains (2:8), but we lack knowledge of any more precise significance of them to the ancient poets, unless we can make something of the word-pairs I pointed out in discussing the earlier appearance of this oath.

It is interesting that the lover is described as a gazelle, leaping over hills and such. And in 2 Sam 2:18 and 1 Chr 12:9 (Engl. 12:8) warriors are described as being swift like gazelles. Whether the gazelle code has only to do with speed has to be uncertain, but that may be a major sense of it. How speedy gazelles are connected with an oath about waking love from sleep is not self-evident. I am fascinated by the statement made by Michael Sells in commenting on Arabic words used in the love elegies of Ibn Arabi, that the Arabic word for gazelle, which occurs there, and which might suggest that Ibn Arabi might have been acquainted with the Song of Songs, is cognate to the Arabic word for love poetry.[1]

The other aspect of the oath is the force of swearing "by" (Hebrew b^e, with, in, by) the animals. I noted in the prior use of this language about the gazelles and deer (2:7) the double senses of the Hebrew words for "gazelles" and "does of the wild," how the words themselves are identical, in the case of "gazelles," or similar in sound, in the case of "does," to frequent terms for the Israelite god. Those similarities to divine words might give us a clue about their use in the oath, using here words as substitutes for the divine ones such as English slang "Heavens" meaning God. There are certainly reasons to associate gazelles and deer with love-gods and -goddesses in that culture and those around it. Carr reproduces several Syrian cylinder-seal portrayals from about 1750 BCE of love-goddesses and gods with figures of what look like gazelles with their curved horns, suggesting a cultural assumption about the animals.[2] The seals are considerably earlier than the Israelite period, but such symbols were doubtless very long-lived in the cultural mind.

---

1. Sells, *Stations of Desire*, 148.
2. Carr, *The Erotic Word*, 112–14.

CH. 3:6–11

מי זאת עלה מן-המדבר כתימרות עשן
מקטרת מר ולבונה מכל אבקת רוכל
הנה מטתו שלשלמה ששים גברים סביב לה
מגברי ישראל
כלם אחזי חרב מלמדי מלחמה
איש חרבו על-ירכו מפחד בלילות
אפריון עשה לו המלך שלמה מעצי הלבנון
עמודיו עשה כסף רפידתו זהב
מרכבו ארגמן תוכו רצוף אהבה
מבנות ירושלם
צאנה וראינה בנות ציון במלך שלמה בעטרה
שעטרה-לו אמו
ביום חתנתו וביום שמחת לבו

{speaker unknown}

[6] Who is this[a] coming up from the desert   like columns of smoke,

fragrant with myrrh and frankincense   from the merchants' powders?

⁷ Well, it is Solomon's litter,   sixty warriors around it,
            Israel's warriors,
    ⁸ all grasping swords,   trained in warfare,
       a sword at each hip   against fears of the night.
⁹ The king made a palanquin,   Solomon, from Lebanese cedar,ᵇ
    ¹⁰ its posts madeᶜ of silver;   its cushions, gold,
       its seats, purple fabric, its interior joined . . .ᵈ Jerusalem's
                                  daughters,ᵉ come out,
            ¹¹ and look, Zion's daughters,
at King Solomon in the crown   with which his mother crowned
                                  him
         on his wedding day,   the day of his heart's joy.

Notes on the translation

a. The opening words, "Who is this," are very strange because "this" is *zo't*, the feminine singular demonstrative pronoun. But no feminine singular referent appears, except Solomon's mother, apparently irrelevant to the subject of the poem. Actually the word for "litter," v. 7, is feminine, but that object could not be referred to as *miy*, "who?," but would have to be called *mah*, "what?" In fact, Exum translates the line as "What is this," without emending *miy* to *mah*.¹ The same phrase occurs at the beginning of a poem in 8:5, "Who is this coming up from the desert?" which goes on to say "leaning upon her lover." There it certainly refers to a female subject. One wonders whether some scribe, coming to this poem, remembered the other and simply put down the wrong gender of "this." Memory can play tricks, even in a culture that depends familiarly on it, though one wonders about proof-reading of the text, which the scribes

1. Exum, *Song of Songs*, 139.

certainly did very carefully. But I will propose a different reading below, without needing to change the text.

b. The parallelism in this couplet may seem confusing in translation. "The king" is parallel to "Solomon," so those two phrases are to be taken as meaning the same person. The rest of the lines are more readily seen as parallel, as "from Lebanese cedar" explains the material of the palanquin in the first line.

c. It is not clear how far the verb "made" reaches, Given the parallelism of "silver" and "gold," we might think that posts and cushions are Solomon's work. On the other hand, the next verb is "joined," v. 10d, and the workers of "joined" seem to be "Jerusalem's daughters." We might think that the fabric work on cushions and seats would all fit the "daughters." I suggest that the latter makes at least as good sense as the alternative, and I propose that by a semi-colon on "silver." Thus, the rest of the materials are supposed to be made by "Jerusalem's daughters."

d. The empty space is filled in Hebrew with the word "love" (*'ah^{a}bah*), which fits very uncomfortably into the sentence without emending it, which I prefer not to do.

e. The only way I have found to bring "Jerusalem's daughters" and "Zion's daughters" into a poetic parallelism that would work is to delete one consonant, the *min* ("by") on the first "daughters," I have declared myself against such changes to the text, and my remaining uncertainty about accepting it is that it results in a very ordinary couplet: "Come out, Jerusalem's daughters and look, Zion's daughters." So neat and convenient. But I am trying to understand and translate poetry, and I am prepared to argue that some generations of copyists probably perpetrated the errors here. I believe this is the only place where I have been constrained (deluded?) into correcting the consonantal Hebrew text, and I will repent at length and leisure.

Commentary

This is the only poem in the collection of which I cannot identify a speaker. It is also the only poem in which Solomon plays a part as an actor, though not as a speaker. The poem moves from subject to subject without making clear the connections among the subjects.

The opening words wonder who the feminine person is, coming with the caravan from the desert. They say "who is this (feminine singular)?" But the only feminine singular human subject mentioned otherwise, is Solomon's mother (v. 11) and we are left to wonder "who" might be meant by "this." I propose that it signifies someone not identified until later, or even never explicitly identified except by implication.

The poem ends with a wedding, of which Solomon is the center. To begin with, I think that Solomon stands for a bridegroom, just as "the king" in the very first poem stands for the lover. And "this" feminine singular person, otherwise not identified, is, I propose, the bride arriving from the desert in state and in safety, accompanied by sixty very well-armed Israelite warriors. Her vehicle, a palanquin, is an enclosed litter with poles by which it is carried by strong men. This one is closely described as having been made of costly materials by Solomon. And at the end, the women of Jerusalem are invited to come out and view "Solomon" on his wedding day. To the presumed woman in the palanquin?

The rest of the verse portrays the palanquin coming up from the desert, sending up dust in clouds that look like smoke. It then moves to the fragrance of the caravan—an image difficult to square with the distance. The sight of what looks like smoke perhaps brings up thoughts of fragrant scents, which will doubtless be received as the caravan approaches.

The caravan is military as vv. 7–8 show, sixty Israelite warriors around Solomon's litter (*miṭṭah*), a word that usually means a bed but in this case stands in for the palanquin. These warriors are strongly armed and well trained for warfare. Each warrior appears to have three swords, one grasped in a hand, the others at each hip. The line "against fears of (literally "in") the night" puts the sole negative feature into the poem. "Against" might be "because of" or "from." But with three swords at close hand for each of the sixty, these warriors are at least ready for trouble and seem to expect it. They surely propose the complete safety of the assumed bride. Perhaps "sixty," a large round number, is even an exaggeration.

At v. 9, the "litter" is called a "palanquin" (*'appiryown*, a word that occurs nowhere else and is apparently borrowed from Greek *phoreion*). A palanquin ordinarily held only one person—fitting for a king or a king's bride—and was carried on poles like a sedan chair. The poet wants us to be interested in its materials and fittings: Lebanese cedar with silver posts, gold cushions (we would think of golden fabric, not gold metal, though the silver-gold parallelism might lead us to think the latter), purple fabric on the seats. At that point the meanings seem to fall apart. "The interior joined" seems all right, but suddenly it is followed by the word for "love," which is sensible in the context only if we suppose that "love" is the mode of joining, at best difficult to understand. We have to move to v. 11 to resume meaningful words.

Suddenly we are in a marriage setting. The women of Jerusalem are summoned to join the festivities and to watch Solomon in his wedding finery. Bridegrooms were, as we have seen before, some-times referred to as kings (1:4, 12), and here is another aspect of that custom: a crown put on the groom's head by his mother. At the end, then, we come to the groom-lover in the person of Solomon, surrounded with all the trappings of royalty. Would the bride, we wonder, have been crowned as well, as she is in some contemporary cultures? Perhaps this poem would have been sung at a wedding celebration, and the entire scene may fit that setting, with the proper poetic exaggeration.

The entire poem may be a complex metaphor for the lover as Solomon, as king, providing his bride with all the trappings of queenship, attendant warriors, richly appointed palanquin, all the local women gathered to see them on "the day of his heart's joy." (And why not "her heart's joy"?)

CH. 4:1–7

הנך יפה רעיתי הנך יפה עיניך יונים
מבעד לצמתך
שערך כעדר העזים שגלשו מהר גלעד
שניך כעדר הקצובות שעלו מן-הרחצה
שכלם מתאימות ושכלה אין בהם
כחוט השני שפתותיך ומדברך נאוה
כפלח הרמון רקתך מבעד לצמתך
כמגדל דויד צוארך בנוי לתלפיות
אלף המגן תלוי עליו כל שלטי הגברים
שני שדיך כשני עפרים תאומי צביה
הרועים בשושנים
עד שיפוח היום ונסו הצללים
אלך לי אל-הר המור ואל-גבעת הלבונה
כלך יפה רעיתי ומום אין בך

The Song of Songs

{he}

4:1 Oh, you are beautiful, love, beautiful, your eyes doves through your veil,

Your hair like a flock of goats drifting down Mt. Gilead,

2 your teeth like shorn ewes coming up from washing,

all with twins, none bereaved;

3 lips like a scarlet thread, lovely your mouth,

cheek like a pomegranate slice through your veil.

4 Like David's tower your neck, built in courses,

a thousand shields hung on it, all warriors' bucklers.

5 Your two breasts like two fawns, twins of a gazelle

grazing among the lilies.

6 Until the day breathes, and the shadows disappear,

I go off to the mountain of myrrh, the hill of frankincense.

7 You are all beautiful, love, no flaw in you.

Commentary

This is the first of three poems that describe a person, part by bodily part, either from top to bottom or from bottom to top. The second is a description of the lover in 5:10–16, and the third, 6:4–10, is again about the woman. Such a descriptive poem has come to be designated *wasf*, from the Arabic word for similar poems in that language. (No, the word has nothing to do with an English term for a stinging insect.) One might wonder if this poem is here as an implicit description if the arriving bride in the prior poem.

Some of the images used are of great interest and totally different from anything in Western poetry. I suspect that no European or American poet has ever described his friend's cheek as "like a pomegranate slice" (v. 3). In order to discuss this image, I bought a pomegranate. It seemed a bit disappointing as an image of beauty: somewhat mildly yellowish meat full of deep red seeds with whitish centers, which covered much more space than the visible meat but gave a strong, variegated texture to the fruit's flesh. The red seeds are the edible element in the whole, and they have a pleasant sweet-sharp taste. Perhaps the pomegranate slice should be considered as a slice just under the skin, which is a rather deep red. Another code: might the word "slice" have signified to a reader or hearer of Hebrew the shape of a cheek? Some other images seem, if anything, even more exotic and unusual: the neck "like David's tower"—how and how much like it, we wonder, and what was David's tower? More codes.

The top-to-bottom order of the description is not uniformly kept. We go from the eyes up to the hair, and then down to the teeth and sideways to the cheek (unless, as some interpreters have it, "cheek" is actually "temple," above the cheeks, which would take us back upwards). Color seems important sometimes, the hair black like a flock of goats, the teeth white like shorn sheep, the lips scarlet. The picturing is quite specific, the hair like a flock of black goats "drifting" down the mountainside, the teeth white like sheep coming up (in the opposite direction) from the washing after being shorn. These similes are again particular to the rural life that these young people knew. Here, without question, it is rural, unlike the city scene we had in 3:1–5. The shorn sheep have lambs in pairs, and in that ancient culture these twin lambs were unusually still together, not taken by wild enemies. So the sheep, like the teeth, are "not bereaved." The natural images persist through the cheeks, compared to a slice of pomegranate. Mixing images is quite typical of this poetry. The poets were not worried about maintaining similar sorts of images in their lists.

But at v. 3e the type of image changes quite drastically. We leave natural images completely. To compare her neck to David's tower, hung with a thousand shields, is an image that can very quickly seem ridiculous. It is impossible to determine just what David's tower was: perhaps a defense or lookout tower of some sort, or an imposing rock formation resembling a tower, called then "David's Tower." It could not be identified today, as there is no indication where it might have been. Clearly another code, but one that the poets meant as a specific site. An earthquake or invasion might in the interim have destroyed it. Ezek 27:11 mentions something being hung on towers, but whether they are shields, as some translations have it, or quivers, according to others, is uncertain. It makes a difference.

On the other hand, do we have another pun? David's name might conceal another word. The name *dawiyd* adds one consonant to *dowd*, "lover" or "love-making," and the name David meant some-thing like "beloved." The tower of love, or the tower of David? That might match its poetic context better, though it is no more identifiable as an object than David's. We can be sure that singers, reciters, or hearers of Hebrew would recognize the similarity between *dawiyd* and *dowd*.

The comparison to a tower suggests, if we are to be literal, that this woman had a very long neck—but literal pictures can quickly become ridiculous. The shields surely point to something like jewelry around the neck. The poem evidently has most to do with how the sights of her affect him, and his exaggeration emphasizes it. Indeed, a thousand warriors' "bucklers" is rather too many for a sensible image, but something about her (or perhaps about him) welcomes his exaggeration.

As to the gazelle and its fawns, it almost seems that her breasts are smaller than usual. Once more, I wish we could have a clearer sense of how the poet would have thought of the connotations of gazelle fawns. It is difficult to decode, given how very unusual this imagery, taken as a whole, is to us in North America, where gazelles do not roam the fields and woods. We will return to a tower of Lebanon to which her nose is compared in 7:5, though I can no more identify the "tower of Lebanon" there than David's tower here, and I must admit the difficulty of understanding comparing her nose to a tower.

It is interesting that the fawns, to which her breasts are compared, are "grazing among the lilies." That phrase elsewhere always refers to an action of the male lover. What it might suggest is at best difficult to understand; perhaps something sexual?

Finally we come to something different, the end of the day, which "breathes" at last. Palestine's summer days were often stifling in heat. The images shift to fragrance with myrrh and frankincense. We have seen them in earlier poems, but they appear in this one only now. Moreover, and perhaps most importantly, the poem is interested in "hills," and that suggests, as it has before, her sexual parts below those previously mentioned.

As we have seen it before, the occurrence of "frankincense" at the end of the poem looks as if it might have functioned as a linking word to the next poem. Frankincense is *l^ebownah*, and Lebanon in the next poem is *l^ebanown*, the similarity of sound between them quite evident. We can understand that the earlier word could function as a reminder to the reciter's or singer's memory of what the next poem is. The same pair of words appears in the poem after the next, in vv. 11, 13, and 15.

CH. 4:8

אתי מלבנון כלה אתי מלבנון תבואי
תשורי מראש אמנה מראש שניר וחרמון
ממענות אריות מהררי נמרים

⁸ With me from Lebanon, bride,ᵃ   with me from Lebanon come,
    journey from the peak of   and of Senir and Chermon,ᵇ
        Amana,
    from lionesses' lair,   leopards' mountains.

Notes on the Translation

a. The change of address from "love" (*ra'yah*, vv. 1 and 7 above) to "bride" (*kallah*) seems to me a reason to identify this as a separate poem.

b. I have transliterated with "Ch" because the first letter of this name is Hebrew *chet*, pronounced as "ch" in Bach. English Bibles generally give the name as Mt. Hermon.

Commentary

This brief poem may be a fragment. As there seems nothing to which we could meaningfully join it, I can think of it only as a very short poem.

The first couplet illustrates something about various kinds of parallelism. Robert Alter refers to this kind of parallelism as "incremental" parallelism.[1] It is partly repetitive: *'ittiy mill^ebanown kallah / 'ittiy mill^ebanown tabow'iy*. The combination of repetition and a continuation of the sentence in the second line makes the parallelism all the more vivid. In addition, the repetition of Lebanon emphasizes a sound link from frankincense (*l^ebownah*) in the prior poem. Another possible name for this kind of parallelism might be "progressive," where the repetition is followed by something new and parallel to the prior part of the expression.

Lebanon, indeed, may be the general term for the three peaks mentioned in the second couplet. Senir and Chermon are two peaks of the same mountain, mentioned in Deut 3:9, and Exum proposes[2] that the three peaks, Amana, Senir, and Chermon, are the middle, northern, and southern parts respectively of the Anti-Lebanon range. This is the only mention in the Hebrew Bible of Amana. In any case, the bride is invited to join her man in coming down from the most impressive mountain range in the entire area.

Its impressiveness is not lessened by identifying it as the locale of lairs of lionesses and leopards. I would like very much to decode the lionesses and leopards. The closest we can come to them, I think, is that both were viewed as dangerous and beautiful wild animals. Exum and Landy[3] both connect animals like this with the woman herself, and Exum especially notes that lions and leopards were associated in Mesopotamian poetry with Ishtar, the goddess of love among other things. That would be enough to suggest a connection of the woman with these animals. As I see this poem as separate, I am quite ready to think of the implications of

---

1. Alter, *The Art of Biblical Poetry*, 188–89.
2. Exum, *Song of Songs*, 169.
3. Ibid.; Landy, *Paradoxes of Paradise*, 137ff.

the wild animals and the woman as an element of wider symbolic connections. The fact that she is leaving the mountains, where the animals are at home, does not suggest giving up the relationship with the goddess. To be sure, we cannot be certain that the Israelite poets knew about Ishtar's connection with lions and leopards. Certainly some folks in Israel would have objected to it, simply because Ishtar was not a goddess to whom Israelites were supposed or allowed to attend. But some Israelites may well have revered Ishtar, or Ashtar or Asherah, Canaanite goddesses of love with names not unlike Ishtar's, and doubtless many who, not knowing about Ishtar, would think of lionesses and leopards as important symbols of the local goddesses.

The poem, then, proposes a journey of the lovers from dangerous peaks and places where there are dangerous but symbolically attractive and important animals. Is the point the safety of the journey's goal or the combinations of beauty and danger in the lovers' being together? As the poem does not refer to the journey's end, the symbols seem to focus on the journey itself. In that case, the possible connection of the animals with a goddess of love and fertility might suggest that, in addition to a connection between women and these animals, they were there to protect the pair of lovers on their journey.

CH. 4:9–15

לבבתני אחותי כלה לבבתיני באחד מעיניך
באחד ענק מצורניך
מה-יפו דדיך אחתי כלה מה-טבו דדיך מיין
וריח שמניך מכל-בשמים
נפת תטפנה שפתותיך כלה דבש וחלב תחת לשונך
וריח שלמתיך כריח לבנון
גן נעול אחתי כלה גל נעול מעין חתום
שלחיך פרדס רמונים עם פרי מגדים
כפרים עם-נרדים נרד וכרכם
קנה וקנמון עם כל-עצי לבונה
מר ואהלות עם כל-ראשי בשמים
מעין גנים באר מים חיים
ונזלים מן-לבנון

⁹ You've taken my heart, sister, bride,   taken my heart with one of your eyes,

one pendant of your necklace.

¹⁰ How fine your loving, sister, bride,   much better than wine,

your perfumes' scent   than any spices.

¹¹ Your lips flow with honey, bride,   honey and milk under your tongue,

your garments' scent   like Lebanon's scent.

¹² A garden^a locked, sister, bride,   a fountain locked, a spring sealed,

¹³ your channels a pomegranate garden   with fine fruits,

henna with nards,   ¹⁴ nard and saffron,

cane and cinnamon   with all the frankincense trees,

myrrh and aloes   with all the finest spices,

¹⁵ a garden spring,^b   a well of fresh water,

flowing down from Lebanon.

Notes on the translation

a. "Garden" and "fountain," in parallel, is also a sound-play: *gan* and *gal*. Whether they always were so close but different is difficult to decide. A number of Hebrew manuscripts and ancient translations have "garden" in both lines. It is easier to understand a scribe's shifting to identical words than introducing a similar but different word. I incline to think, on the principal that the more difficult reading is the more likely correct one, that "spring," therefore, is original Moreover, not only does "spring" appear in v. 15 but it appears along with "garden."

b. Literally, "a spring (or fountain) of gardens." I take the plural "gardens" as an abstraction.

Commentary

The opening verb is interesting for more than one reason: *libbabtini*, a rare verb derived from *leb*, "heart," which I translate "taken my heart," may be nearest to "you have heartened me." I interpret that to mean her controlling his heart, though "hearten" usually means to uphold and strengthen the heart's courage. Some interpreters read it as "seduced."[1] I come closer to Exum's "captured my heart"[2], though I find the thought more like "governed." She has control of his thought and therefore of his decisions. Moreover, the word *libbabtiniy* has several sounds in common with "Lebanon" and *lebownah*, "frankincense," the former in 4:8, 11, and perhaps acting as a linking word, and "frankincense" in this poem at v. 14.

I think we should consider that the verb "loving" in the following line means more like "love-making" than what we might think of as "heart-felt" loving, by which we mean the emotions of loving. I don't mean to suggest that they did not feel love, but it appears that they located that feeling bodily not in the chest, as we do, but in the bowels, lower down in the body. And in any case, the heart (*lebab*) keeps up plays of sounds with *l*'s and *b*'s.

There is a kind of desirable helplessness in the man's sense of being taken over, controlled, by his beloved, "with (only) one of your eyes," and only one pendant of the necklace. This proceeds to a catalog poem of natural things that now signify loving to him: tastes, smells, natural sights; spices, gardens, waters. It begins with seeing her, her eyes and then her necklace, and proceeds to her touch in the acts of loving. Then follows a constant shift back and forth between taste and scent: wine and perfumes and spices; honey and milk and the scent of garments and of Lebanon (presumably the rich smell of cedar). At v. 13 it is back to taste: pomegranates

1. Landy, *Paradoxes of Paradise*, 98–99.
2. Exum, *Song of Songs*, 154.

and fruit; and smell: henna, nard, saffron. Again taste: cane, cinnamon (alliterative in Hebrew: *qanah* and *qinnamown*); smell: frankincense, myrrh, aloes, spices. The inventiveness—indeed, sexiness—of these lists in this catalog is poetically impressive.

Finally the garden spring, the well, and a resumption of the Lebanon mountain landscape from the prior poem provide another possible linking factor. All the refreshment of taste, smell, and sight returns at the very end of the catalog. The repetitions of these factors and their differences are remarkably successful.

I keep thinking of links among poems rather than only of the continuation of images. And that suggests to me again ways in which the poems might have been brought orally into collections and have been presented in recitation or song. Another instance of linking is the way *gan*, "garden," is connected to *gan* in the following poem at 4:16c and e and 5:1.

CH. 4:16—5:1

עורי צפון ובואי תימן
הפיחי גני יזלו בשמיו
יבא דודי לגנו ויאכל פרי מגדיו
באתי לגני אחתי כלה אריתי מורי אם-בשמי
אכלתי יערי עם-דבשי שתיתי ייני עם-חלבי
אכלו רעים שתו ושכרו דודים

{she}

¹⁶ Wake up, north wind,   come, south wind,
    breathe on my garden,   flowing forth its spices.
My lover comes to his garden   and eats its fine fruits.

{he}

5:¹ I come to my garden,   pick my[a] myrrh with spice,
    sister, bride.
eat honeycomb with honey,   drink wine with milk.

{daughters}

Eat, friends,   drink, be drunk on loving.[b]

THE SONG OF SONGS

Notes on the Translation

a. In each of the first lines of 5:1, all of the nouns have the possessive pronoun "my." I kept it in the translation of the first, but omitted it in the rest as more repetitive than is comfortable in English, and as implied by the first use.

b. The Hebrew *dowdiym* might mean either "lovers" (masc, plural) or "lovings" in the sense of multiple acts of love. The former would give us parallelism with "friends" (*re'iym*), and "drink, be drunk, lovers." I think "loving" makes better sense, though there is no word for "on" in the line. Perhaps "Be drunk loving" would have served.

Commentary

This dialogue poem is spoken in v. 16 by the woman, in 5:1 by the man, and the final couplet by "Jerusalem's daughters." So many links from the prior poem might suggest that the two poems are actually one. The garden imagery recalls the previous poem, "fine fruits" is repeated from there, as are honeycomb, honey, myrrh, and the spices. In fact, this entire poem continues the main images of the other. The same shifts of image from scent to taste to sight occur here. The principal changes are the winds at the beginning, references to wine and milk, and the injection in the last couplet of the urging to love, doubtless to be thought of as spoken by the chorus of daughters.

The first stanza, spoken by the woman, is all about preparation of the garden for the lover to come. She invites the winds to come and bring the spices to life. She calls the garden both "my" garden and "his" garden, though she seems to be in charge of it, while the lover eats the "fine fruits." In 5:1, the lover describes his preparations for love-making in eating aphrodisiac foods and spices, which echo the "fine fruits" of the woman's speech. He also echoes her mention of the garden's possessors, calling it "my" garden. The combinations may be odd, myrrh combined with spice, wine drunk with milk. One might think of these connections as playful, perhaps even bizarre. The encouragement to making love by the bystanding "daughters" continues the focus on eating and drinking, though what is drunk is love.

CHS. 5:2—6:3

אני ישנה ולבי ער קול דודי דופק
פתחי-לי אחתי רעיתי יונתי תמתי
שראשי נמלא-טל קווצותי רסיסי לילה
פשטתי את-כתנתי איככה אלבשנה
רחצתי את-רגלי איככה אטנפם
דודי שלח ידו מן-החר ומעי המו עליו
קמתי אני לפתח לדודי וידי נטפו-מור
ואצבעתי מור עבר על כפות המנעול
פתחתי אני לדודי ודודי חמק עבר
נפשי יצאה בדברו
בקשתיהו ולא מצאתיהו קראתיו ולא ענני
מצאני השמרים הסבבים בעיר
הכוני פצעוני
נשאו את-רדידי מעלי שמרי החמות
השבעתי אתכם בנות ירושלם
אם-תמצאו את-דודי מה-תגידו לו
שחולת אהבה אני
מה-דודך מדוד היפה בנשים

The Song of Songs

מה-דודך מדוד שככה השבעתנו
דודי צח ואדום דגול מרבבה
ראשו כתם פז קוצותיו תלתלים
שחרות כעורב

עיניו כיונים על-אפיקי מים
רחצות בחלב ישבות על-מלאת
לחיו כערוגת הבשם

מגדלות מרקחים
שפתותיו שושנים נטפות מור עבר
ידיו גלילי זהב ממלאים בתרשיש
מעיו עשת שן מעלפת ספירים
שוקיו עמודי שש מיסדים על-אדני-פז
מראהו כלבנון בחור כארזים
חכו ממתקים וכלו מחמדים
זה דודי וזה רעי בנות ירושלם
אנה הלך דודך היפה בנשים
אנה פנה דודך ונבקשנו עמך
דודי ירד לגנו לערוגות הבשם
לרעות בגנים וללקט שושנים
אני לדודי ודודי לי הרעה בשושנים

² I was asleep, my heart awake— the sound—my lover's knocking!

{he}

Open the door, sister, love, my dove, my perfect one.

My hair is soaked with dew, my locks with night's damp.

{she}

³ I have taken off my robe, how can I put it on?

I have washed my feet, how can I dirty them?ᵃ

⁴ My lover put his hand into the lock— my stomach churned because of

I got up to open for my lover, my hands dripping with myrrh,

fingers flowing myrrh on the handles of the bolt.

⁶ I opened to my lover— he had turned and gone.

I couldn't breathe because of him.ᵇ

I looked for him but couldn't find him, called but he didn't answer.

⁷ The guards found me, who patrol around the city,

beat me, wounded me, stripped off my cloak,

those guardians of the walls.

⁸ I put you on oath, Jerusalem's daughters, if you find my lover—

what should you tell him?— that I'm faint with love.

{daughters}

⁹ What is your lover more than any lover, most beautiful woman?ᶜ

What is your lover more than any lover, that you give us such an oath?

The Song of Songs

{she}

¹⁰ My lover is shiny and ruddy, a banner above ten thousand,
¹¹ his head pure gold, his locks palm spathes,
Black[d] as a raven,
¹² his eyes like doves on channels of water,
bathed in milk, sitting over a full stream.
¹³ His cheeks like beds of balsam, towers of spices,
his lips lilies, dripping myrrh.
¹⁴ his hands golden circles filled with beryl,
his belly an ivory plaque, covered with sapphires,
¹⁵ his legs marble pillars, set in golden bases,
his appearance like Lebanon, standing out like the cedars,
¹⁶ his mouth is sweetness, and he is utterly desirable.
This is my lover, this my friend, Jerusalem's daughters.

{daughters}

6:¹ Where did your lover go, most beautiful woman?[c]
Where did your lover turn? We'd like to search for him with you

{she}

² My lover went down to his garden, to the beds of balsam,
to enjoy himself in the gardens, and to pick the lilies.
³ I am my lover's, and my lover is mine. He grazes among the lilies.

THE SONG OF SONGS

Notes on the Translation

a. The first and third lines of this verse have verbs in the perfect tense, and the verbs in the alternating lines are imperfects. Many translations have these lines spoken by the woman to herself, but it seems to make best sense that she speaks them to the man. Thus I translate the perfects as English present perfects and the other verbs as presents with "can."

b. The Hebrew $b^e dabb^e ro$, "Because of what he said," makes no sense in the context. Exum, following Fox, makes the sensible change of vowels to $bidbaro$, "on his account, because of him."[1]

c. In both v. 9 and 6:1, the phrase in Hebrew is "most beautiful of women."

d. Palm spathes, sheathing bracts, are black, as Exum points out[2] Marcia Falk solved it by leaving out the palm entirely and translating "black like wings of ravens."[3]

Commentary

Exactly what the first line means is, to put it mildly, debatable. Was she dreaming? That is surely one explanation. Exum[4] has a more subtle account: it is the moment between sleeping and waking, hearing something that one thinks may be a dream but also may have been heard on waking. There is a dreamlike quality to this entire poem, which is the longest in the book, but it is so vivid and detailed that it is difficult to explain the entire poem as a dream. Difficult for me, at any rate: but I find remembering my dreams very hard.

There he is, speaking urgently to wake her. We may be mildly amused at his piling up terms of endearment, ending with "my

1. Exum, *Song of Songs*, 185.
2. Ibid, 204.
3. Falk, *Love Lyrics from the Bible*, poem 19, 3rd page.
4. Exum, *Song of Songs*, 193.

perfect one," and his almost frantic insistence on being let in out of the wet. Poor fellow! She is almost too resistant, if anything, having to put on clothes again, getting her clean feet dirty. How can he be so demanding?

But then he puts his hand "into" the lock. The preposition is actually "from," and "lock" is one interpretation of the word, which means basically "hole." But "from" can in some contexts mean "in" or even "into," and that seems to be the sense here. If the hole meant "lock," it is not very helpful as information about locks on the doors of Israelite houses. The entire scene may not be of a lock at all. We need to recall that "hand" (*yad*) in Hebrew is sometimes a euphemism for "penis," and the sexual meaning of "hole" is quite unmistakable. When she goes on to say that her stomach "churned" because of him, it is a short step to thinking of the episode as sexual from beginning to end. Even the expression in v. 2 that I translated as "open the door" does not have the word "door" in Hebrew but only "open to me." So we may be reading euphemisms from the outset. That renders the notion of dreaming, if anything, even more attractive—but not attractive enough for me simply to adopt it.

The verb "open" in vv. 5–6 has no noun after it. But the shock has come: the lover has gone. Was she too slow to respond to his wishes? Perhaps that was really only a "hand" that went into a "hole" in the door, and her stomach "churned" in anticipation. What can you do with a text that presents you sometimes with euphemisms and sometimes not? One of the things you can do is to figure out what it might mean in either case.

She apparently goes off in a vain search for him (v. 6d-e). But the watchmen in the city have a successful search, and this issues in a piece of unnecessary and excessive violence. In the prior search through the city (3:1–4), she met the watchmen and got away with only a question to them, which they did not answer. Here they seem to be upholding the public morality with what can seem to us only an immoral thuggery: stripping and beating. Where she was unwilling to put on clothes for her lover, the watchmen compel taking off her clothes. The unusual factor in this narrative is that no comment is made about that except the after-thought, perhaps intended as savagely ironic: "those guardians of the walls." How dangerous to the walls was she? I translated the same word at the beginning of v. 7 as "watchmen"—and *šomer* can mean both watchman and guardian, but in the present line they were acting dreadfully as guardians. In fact, we must be surprised that the watchmen didn't rape her. But perhaps they did, and she didn't report it. Or perhaps it was a dream that didn't include rape—can psychiatrists explain that?

Now begins a dialogue with Jerusalem's daughters, that frequent chorus. She wants them to find her lover and tell him (presumably) what has happened. Or is that not the wish? It is a dramatic point. "If you find him, tell him—what?" That she was caught, stripped, and beaten? No? Why not? Perhaps she wants to tell him that herself, though in the event she does not. "What shall you tell him? That I'm faint with love."

It seems that the women have no clue to what has happened. They are interested only in the lover and want to know how he is more than any other lover. Is that an "all men are the same" remark? It is surely an invitation for her to tell them why he is not like any lover. And yet, what she tells them is a portrait, unusually in the form of a *wasf*, of a man very much like many men, though perhaps more so, a man viewed through the eyes of a woman in love with him. Yet what she sees is doubtless not unlike what the "daughters" would see if they could see him.

The description follows from the top of his head to his feet (v. 15b), and returning to his mouth. Some of it is unusual and difficult to clarify. A "pure gold" head with raven-black hair is at best not descriptively clear. In fact, she uses two words for gold (*ketem paz*), both of which mean gold, and I take the apposition to be emphatic and expansive. If a Palestinian man with yellow hair seems the next thing to impossible, might it mean a sun-tanned face? Perhaps more likely the gold images are emotional description, not pictorial. Why the black hair is described as palm spathe, a sheathing bract, and what the bract sheathes is not certain. Palm spathes are, in fact, apparently black, and hair does sheathe at least part of a head.

Her eyes were described as "doves" in 1:15 and 4:1, and I am uncertain how to decode the dove. Eyes like doves that sit by water might refer to milky eyeballs. We think of doves as gentle birds, but we cannot know that that is the quality intended here. These four lines are difficult to sort out. Perhaps a series of poets was carried away by the description of the eyes, and some of the phrases, especially those having to do with water, are all but impossible to understand.

The kinds of similes and metaphors vary from part to part. Cheeks are like beds of spices but also like towers—a picture very hard to draw, and I think these poets seldom thought visually—lips like flowers, hands precious metals, belly precious stones. His legs are marble, his feet gold. All of this has to do with her perception of his qualities, and much less with what it all actually looks like. The man's descriptions of the woman in his *wasfs* are more nearly pictorial than this. What could she mean by a belly covered with sapphires? It can hardly mean anything except that she finds him very desirable. She is not picturing him but connecting with him. I do not believe that by comparing him to Lebanon she thinks of him as a mountain, or by referring to cedars she means forests. He stands for everything impressive and valuable. And that becomes clear at v. 16a–b: "his mouth is sweetness and all of him desirable." So, women of Jerusalem, now you know who this lover is.

The last section of the poem is a fascinating exercise in restraint. The listening chorus responds to this remarkable description, in effect, "Where can we find this bewitching fellow? We'll look for him with you." Her answer is a lovely piece of stonewalling: "He has gone to his garden," meaning, of course, "he belongs to me, and you can't get there." Clearly this garden is the woman herself, and she has no intention of sharing him with anybody. She has him all, knows what she has, and is quite prepared to be possessive. Perhaps the whole thing teases the "daughters" by being pure fantasy—and they fall for it.

The Song of Songs

Thinking about the relation of this poem to the earlier one about the night search for her lover makes me wonder whether the two poems might have derived from a single original. To paraphrase Robert Frost, "Two poems diverged in some poets' minds." The first is considerably shorter and emerges as rather benign, an experience of searching for and finding a lover in the city at night. The second emerged as a much more detailed poem, also about searching for a lover in the city at night, but beginning with the lover's coming to her place and leaving before she could let him in (if that is what it means) and continuing to an encounter with the thuggish watchmen ostensibly guarding Jerusalem's walls. That she found the lover takes a quite different turn from the discovery in the other poem, and proceeds to detailed conversation with the "daughters," including that extensive *wasf* describing him. The shorter first poem might have been closer to the original, and the second was strongly elaborated but included several features common to both, along with the mildly humorous cover-up in the conclusion to the "daughters." That an original poem, which I cannot reconstruct, might have developed separately into two very dissimilar poems in the process of transmission strikes me as an interesting comment on orally transmitted poetry.

CH. 6:4–10

יפה את רעיתי כתרצה נאוה כירושלם
אימה כנדגלות
הסבי עיניך מנגדי שהם הרהיבני
שערך כעדר העזים שגלשי מן-הגלעד
שניך כעדר הרחלים שעלו מן-הרחצה
שכלם מתאימות ושכלה אין בהם
כפלח הרמון רקתך מבעד לצמתך
ששים המה מלכות ושמנים פילגשים
ועלמות אין מספר
אחת היא יונתי תמתי אחת היא לאמה
ברא היא ליולדתה
ראוה בנות ויאשרוה מלכות ופילגשים ויהללוה
מי-זאת הנשקפה כמו-שחר יפה כלבנה
ברה כחמה אימה כנדגלות

The Song of Songs

{he}

⁴ You are beautiful as Tirzah, my love, lovely as Jerusalem

awesome as those marvels.

⁵ Turn your eyes from me, they're too much for me;

your hair like a flock of goats that drifts down from Gilead;

⁶ your teeth like shorn ewes coming up from the washing,

all with twins, and none bereaved.

⁷ Like a slice of pomegranate your cheek through your veil.[a]

⁸ There are sixty queens, eighty concubines

innumerable young women;

⁹ only one[b] is she, my perfect dove, only one to her mother,

pure to the one who bore her.

Daughters,[c] seeing her, call her blessed, queens and concubines praise her.

¹⁰ Who is this[d] looking down like dawn, beautiful as the moon,

pure as the hot sun, awesome as those marvels?

Notes on the translation

a. Vv. 5b–7 is almost identical to 4:1d-2, 3c-d. Such repetitions are not otherwise unknown in the book, though they are not frequent. They may be another indication of oral transmission, where phrases or even groups of lines have been used in more than one setting.

b. "Only" is not there in Hebrew, and I inserted it because "one" is surely in contrast to "sixty" and "eighty"; the same is true of "only" in the next line.

c. "Daughters" is literal and it could be translated "women." The Song often uses "daughters" in this kind of setting, and I have tended to be literal about them. "Young women" in v. 8c is not "daughters" but *ᵃlamot*, "young women, girls" as in 1:3.

d. "Who is this" uses the feminine singular demonstrative, "this." The following adjectives, "pure" and "awesome" are also feminine singular. The obvious subject is the loved woman.

Commentary

Not often does one find a comparison of a woman's beauty to a city—let alone two of them, both capitals. Tirzah was briefly the capital of the northern kingdom, Israel, after Solomon's death, until Omri, then King of Israel, moved the capital about fifty years later to Samaria. This is the only mention of Tirzah's beauty, and it may be here only to have a pair of cities including Jerusalem. The fact that Tirzah had ceased to be a capital a long time before the poem took its final shape may not matter. At the same time, the mention of Tirzah's beauty might suggest that the poem had its origin at a time when Tirzah still was or recently had been Israel's capital. By the time the Song of Songs was taking its final shape, Jerusalem was not the capital of Judah, as it had been, but a major city in territory occupied by a foreign power. Jerusalem had been described as beautiful in a number of places elsewhere in the Hebrew Bible.

The poet uses a word, *'eymah*, that I translated twice, in the third line (where it is spelled *'ayumah*) and in the last line of the poem, as "awesome." I have been reminded that "awesome" has been trivialized in adolescent street talk in the United States to mean something like "OK" or "swell." I refuse to relinquish the word. It includes, as does the Hebrew word, the thought of frighteningly impressive strength, something that calls for a response of "awe." That sense in "awesome" gives voice to the ancient poet who said or sang a feeling of awe before the subject, not once but twice. When modern youths say "awesome" they are not thinking of impressive strength but of something "pretty good."

So beauty for this poet is not merely a "marvel" but something disturbing as well. "Turn your eyes from me" expresses that consideration, though the rest of the description does not emphasize disturbance. Indeed, right through v. 7 we are hearing words almost precisely the same as in 4:1–3, here as a kind of semi-*wasf*, which seems to focus on color or shade, black like goats, white like washed sheep, reddish like sliced pomegranate. It suggests again a re-use in oral form as we have seen such things before. Some of the descriptive material in this poetry has to do with sight and especially with color. That strikes me as unusual; descriptive language in the Hebrew Bible seems remarkably lacking in the use of colors in description. Even the famous "coat of many colors" in the King James Version of Gen. 37:3 turns out on more modern linguistic investigation to have been a "long robe with sleeves" (RSV, NRSV) though the NJPS translation says "an ornamented robe."

He (the man is the speaker) goes on to talk about women's positions of power, as queens and concubines—the latter surely functioning in royal courts. Where these sixty queens are to be found is not revealed, nor are they described as attached to Solomon, whose harem was defined in 1 Kgs as considerably larger than this. To be sure, our sixty queens match the sixty warriors from Solomon's military force in 3:7. Still, they are simply queens and concubines and "innumerable young women." Perhaps the numbers sixty and eighty are codes with significance known to the ancient Israelites, but the number is clearly in opposition to the beloved woman, who is only one. And in her case, one is absolutely enough, for him, for her mother, and for anyone else who may be involved, including queens and royal concubines.

The poem then closes with more beauty and more "marvels," which are the beloved woman, compared to dawn, sun, and moon. With a fine sense of completion, it ends with the same line as the last in the first tercet. She, then, is as awesomely beautiful as the famous cities and, moreover, as the sun and moon. "Who is this" indeed (v. 10a)? But we know and instinctively we believe. She is the "one" beyond all others.

CH. 6:11–12

אל-גנת אגוז ירדתי לראות באבי הנחל
לראות הפרחה הגפן הנצו הרמנים
לא ידעתי נפשי שמתני מרכבות עמי-נדיב

{she}

¹¹ I went down to the nut orchard   to look at the valley's blossoms,

to see whether the vines had bloomed,   the pomegranates were in flower.

¹² [I didn't know myself . . .   chariots my noble people.]ᵃ

Notes on the Translation

a. The last couplet is corrupted and makes no sense after the first three Hebrew words. "Chariots," "my people," and "noble" can be read in the last line but not in a way that helps us to form a sentence. The verb under the ellipsis in the first line has something to do with "setting," but in what way is completely uncertain, and I have simply omitted the word from further consideration. More discussion below. I find nothing in this couplet that leads me to think that it continues the preceding lines or connects with the following ones. I suppose that some serious miscopying took place, and I prefer not to attempt its repair.

Commentary

It seems almost an invasion to try to read a very brief partial poem, which is what we apparently have here. The Hebrew-less reader will not be helped by seeing the Hebrew of the last couplet, and I have translated as much of it as I find intelligible. The reader in control of Hebrew may see why I find no meaning in it: *lo' yada'tiy napšiy samatniy mark^{e}bowt 'ammiy-nadiyb*. The last, hyphenated words might be a name, Ammiynadiyb, which occurs only here, though it is like Amminadab, the name of two men, one a member of the tribe of Judah, the father of Aaron's wife, and the other a Levite mentioned in Chronicles. This does not help with our words, not even though Amminadab is found in some Hebrew manuscripts, the Septuagint (Greek), and the Latin Vulgate. I conclude that either Ammiynadiyb is a name otherwise unknown, or it is supposed to mean something. "My kinsman is noble (or perhaps willing)," a possible meaning, fails to say anything useful to me, and to prefix that by "The chariots of" solves nothing. But the fact that *nadiyb* occurs again toward the beginning of the next poem, "noble daughter," 7:2b, makes it a possible linking word.

There is no clue to the speaker's gender in the opening couplets; it describes a stroll in the country to look at blossoms, mentions the nut orchard, the vines, and the pomegranates. The time seems to be spring. We have seen something of the code of vines, which appears to be sexual, and pomegranates suggest the same area, without being as distinct. The rest of the book is more interested in the fruit than the blossoms of the pomegranate. As for the nut orchard, this is its only mention in the book, and the kind of nuts cannot be recovered. Sometimes a collection of poems will have one, like this, that seems less than readily comprehensible, even now and then in a collection whose author we know and who wrote in our own language. I regret my inability to shed more light on what seems a partial little poem.

CH. 7:1–10

שובי שובי השולמית שובי שובי ונחזה-בך
מה-תחזו בשולמית כמחלת המחנים
מה-יפו פעמיך בנעלים בת-נדיב
חמוקי ירכיך כמו חלאים מעשה ידי אמן
שררך אגן הסהר אל-יחסר המזג
בטנך ערמת חטים סוגה בשושנים
שני שדיך כשני עפרים תאמי צביה
צוארך כמגדל השן עיניך ברכות בחשבון
על-שער בת-רבים
אפך כמגדל הלבנון צופה פני דמשק
ראשך עליך ככרמל ודלת ראשך כארגמן
מלך אסור ברהטים
מה-יפית ומה-נעמת אהבה בתענוגים
זאת קומתך דמתה לתמר ושדיך לאשכלות
אמרתי אעלה בתמר אחזה בסנסניו
ויהיו-נא שדיך כאשכלות הגפן
וריח אפך כתפוחים
וחכך כיין הטוב הולך לדודי למישרים
דובב שפתי ישנים

The Song of Songs

{men (?)}

¹ Turn,ᵃ turn, Shulammite,ᵇ   turn, turn, so we can gaze at you.

{she}

How are youᶜ gazing at the Shulammite,   like a dance between two camps?

{he}

² How beautiful your stepsᵈ in sandals, noble daughter,

your thighs' curves like jewels, the work of artistic hands;

³ between themᵉ a rounded bowl, that never lacks mixed wine;

your belly a heap of wheat hedged by lilies;

⁴ your two breasts like two fawns, a gazelle's twins,

⁵ your neck like an ivory tower, your eyes pools in Heshbon,

by the gate of Bath-Rabbim,ᶠ

your nose like the tower of Lebanon looking over to Damascus;

⁶ your head like Carmel, and its hair like purple,

a king is bound in your tresses.

⁷ How beautiful you are and how delightful, love, with pleasures.

⁸ Your form like a palm tree, your breasts date-clusters.

⁹ I think I'll climb the palm, take hold of its clusters.

Your breasts are like bunches of grapes, the scent of your nose like apples;

¹⁰ your cheeks like the best wine, flowing smoothly to lovers,

gliding to sleepers' lips.

The Song of Songs

Notes on the translation

a. The verb can also mean "to come back" or "return." I take "turn" as having something to do with the "dance" in v. 1d, though Exum[1] denies that it can have that meaning.

b. Some scholars generalize Shulammite almost as the woman's name, though this is the only place where she is called that. The word Shulammite (*shuwlammiyt*) is similar to "Solomon" (*sh^{e}lomo*), which may have something to do with its meaning. I doubt that Shulammite is a name, but it might designate a feminine "Solomonite," though what that might mean is not at all clear.

c. "You" is masculine plural, suggesting that the unidentified speaker(s), "we," of the first couplet is a group of men. "How" implies something like ""in what way are you gazing?" which might make us wonder whether the gaze is respectful or not. But the word could also verge into "why?" or "for what reason?"

d. The word has to do with feet, though it is usually less like feet as bodily parts than like things feet do. I leave it as more literal.

e. The word is rare and uncertain. Exum[2] notes an Arabic cognate, for which vulva is one meaning, but, like other translators, she uses "navel," which looks like an effort to avoid "vulva." But "navel" intrudes on "belly" in the next couplet. I conclude to translate with an expression that proposes the vulva but for reasons set out below, does not use the word.

f. The location of the gate of Bath-Rabbim (meaning "Daughter of Many"), no doubt in the city of Heshbon, is unknown.

Commentary

The speaker in the first couplet is uncertain. The masculine plural "you" in the next verse suggests that the first couplet is spoken

1. Exum, *Song of Songs*, 225.
2. Ibid., 213.

by a group of men. Who they might have been is unknown, and the man who speaks later is certainly by himself. But her response to this first exhortation to "turn," mentions the "dance between two camps," which is not immediately meaningful. "Camps" is unusual in being in the dual number, thus meaning specifically two of them, though a place named Mahanaim ("two camps") plays a role in both Genesis and 2 Samuel. This poem has plenty of place names, and I incline against identifying this as another. "Camp" ordinarily designates a military installation, not what we would call "going camping." The dance seems to be almost a way to separate the camps from each other, perhaps averting conflict between them. That might propose that the "How?" or "Why?" could be a suggestion about keeping the two camps separate by her dance. We might also think of the two "camps" as two sets of wishful lovers, which would attract a "dance" to encourage them.

The military sense seems to disappear immediately as the man proceeds to describe her in another *wasf*, that poetic genre describing someone part by bodily part. We have seen two of them, describing the woman in 4:1–5 and the man in 5:10–16. Here we come to a different description of the woman. Watching women dance might have been popular entertainment at military camps and certainly where groups of men gathered to get closer to their women friends.

This *wasf* covers (or uncovers) the body in the opposite direction from the earlier one on the woman, here beginning at her feet and ending with her head. Like the one on the man's body, this one has a varied collection of images, mostly similes, some comparing her to natural factors like wheat or animals, some to manufactured goods like jewelry or wine, some to architectural objects such as towers. I see no particular order or pattern to the images. Their variety might look like the result of improvisation—another element suggesting oral composition. Some of them are not similes but the first one, on her feet, is simply descriptive. The noun really is "steps" and may be intended to call attention to what the feet are doing in their sandals. Her "steps" are "beautiful." Not an immensely imaginative line. But the adjective with "daughter" here is *nadiyb*, which reminds us as a linking word of the uncertain *'ammiynadiyb*, "my noble people," at the end of 6:12.

The quality of imagination improves as we move upwards on her body. Jewel-like curves of thighs is somewhat unclear, especially as it leaves aside any soft texture to the thigh, but emphasizes color, shape, and value. The "rounded bowl" with "mixed wine" emphasizes shape, perhaps scent, and taste. But why, we might wonder, mixed wine? Surely it refers to a highly desirable wine, perhaps in a metaphor for the mixing of sexual juices.

Some translators read "vulva" for "navel," but Exum finds an Arabic cognate to the Hebrew word used here (see n. 33). I find "vulva" inappropriately specific. English sexual terms tend to be either explicitly technical and often Latinate words, such as "vulva" or "penis," or more casual words that are hardly more than pornographic slang, with few if any possible choices between the two types. I have stepped away from the defining words of either kind and prefer, after the line about thighs, "between them," i.e., the thighs, which seems to me accurate enough that we know what body part is meant and also less than objectionably precise, allowing the metaphor of the bowl of mixed wine full force. And it frees us from fussing about the precise meaning of the word that is there, even if we are quite sure what that meaning is, or ought to be. I don't think that turns me into a prissy Victorian.

The belly as "heap of wheat" might suggest a rounded shape, and also the color of the wheat. Modern preferences for slender, flat tummies do not necessarily match what was taken as beauty in the ancient world, where people might have liked evidence of hearty eating. Another code, as is the next image. Exactly what hedging lilies stand for is not certain, though I wonder whether they may have something to do with pubic hair. To be sure, lilies are ordinarily the wrong color. Still, men are very much drawn to women's pubic hair, and comparing it to lilies does not surprise me. It might have nothing to do with color, perhaps entirely with texture or with some other familiar association. We are dealing again with a code, the specific connotations of which to the ancients are not available to us. Recalling the phrase, used about men, "grazing among the lilies," we may think that the metaphor is an unusual description of a man's sexual activity, though perhaps reference to sexual play with a woman's pubic parts, as Alter proposes,[3] is excessively literal decoding of the phrase. Metaphors are not necessarily precisely descriptive. Their suggestivity widens their possible applications.

At v. 4 we come back to the fawn-gazelle code, one of the favorite images in these poems. Is that reference to the color of beige animals and of their grace? It is difficult to be sure of these connotations, and especially so frequent a combination as this one. It occurs six other times in the book: at 2:7, 9, 17; 3:5; 4:5; and 8:14. Sometimes it is in the woman's voice, sometimes in the man's. Here, as in 4:5, the man is comparing her breasts to the animals, and I think we should keep in mind that the description is in the mouth of a man in love with the described woman. In 2:7 and 3:5, she requires the group of women to swear an oath on them. In 2:9 and 17 she compares him to the animals, and in 8:14 she urges him to "flee away" like them, in a line that does not seem to mean a frightened escape but only a swift one.

Linking her eyes to pools is uncertain. I incline to think the image is not color, but has something to do with the liquid around the eyes, which reminds the onlooker of pools. These pools are specifically in Heshbon, near the gate of Bath-Rabbim, whatever and wherever that was. We may assume it was in Heshbon, a city across the Jordan that passed back and forth to and from Amorites, Moabites, and Israelites for some time. Isa 6:8–10 mentions vineyards and fertile fields in Heshbon, but we must remain in the dark about the gate, Bath-Rabbim ("daughter of many" or of chiefs). Exum thinks that Heshbon might have had an exotic connotation for the poets,[4] and its long past as a capital of other tribes and groups could support such an idea.

When we come to her nose, we must think again that this was a "towering" woman. Her neck was described in v. 5 as "like an ivory tower"—natural or human-made?—and now her nose

---

3. Alter, *The Art of the Biblical Poetry*, 197–98.
4. Exum, *Song of Songs*, 235.

is compared to a (or the) "tower of Lebanon." Again, the thought might be of a natural rock formation or of something humanly constructed. It is an unusual comparison to a woman's nose, unless the point has more to do with its "looking over to Damascus" than its shape or size. The image is not clear, and some commentators find it simply ridiculous. But in these poems Lebanon is often involved with scents, especially of cedars, and the nose, of course, may suggest that. At the same time, Lebanon is frequently an image of high, impressive mountains and mountain ranges. Still, our puzzling over decoding the image suggests that it is less than successful for us, however successful it might have been for the ancient singers and hearers of the poem. We should probably try to avoid lessening the oddities of the images. They are theirs, not ours, and we are responsible to their thoughts.

Yet the image may be related to the next one, comparing her head to Carmel, an important hill in northern Israel on the Mediterranean coast. The geography of this poem skips long distances from place to place. Carmel is very far from Heshbon and from Damascus. But the poet is clearly fascinated with geographical shapes in the general area of the Lebanon mountains. Perhaps comparing her head to Carmel indicates that the hill might have been tree-covered, an apt comparison to hair.

The imagery changes in vv. 7–10, so completely that we must wonder whether we are in a new poem. It has to do with her body, first as a palm tree, which he wishes to climb, and then various parts of it to other plant types. The palm is climbable, and any boy worth his salt would like to try. Breasts as date-clusters is an unusual image, surely not referring to shapes or to colors, but perhaps to taste and continuing the reference to palms. Date clusters tend to be bunches of small ovoid shapes, and are on the whole dark colors. Does this hark back to "I am black and beautiful"? How are breasts like that? Well, it seems, they aren't, unless they were allowed to be browned by the sun. Again, the code is elusive. Perhaps the details are less important than the thought of clambering up a woman's body for whatever rewards are there for you.

Immediately, of course, the simile changes to the poem's third metaphor for breasts. The breasts are no longer like fawns (v. 4) or like date-clusters but like bunches of grapes, a less-than-successful pictorial image, surely having no connection to a palm tree. What are the poets thinking about? Taste? Scent? Smooth textures of skin? All of those would fit dates and grapes, and the apples in the following line might suggest scent here. Still, the comparisons seem somewhat forced, if also adventuresome. Other comparisons to scents (her nose like apples) and taste (wine), reaching with its distinctive smoothness to lips might suggest a series of metaphorical suggestions. It is surely very sexy, taking us to places where we seldom go in ways by which we seldom get there. Perhaps they were having some fun with these different and differing images—"Let's see how these strike them!" We don't often think of ancient people as "having fun," but I think we should give that idea much more play. The Song of Songs surely portrays ancient people having fun.

A Brief Diversion On "Turn"

At four places in preceding poems the image of "turning" is important. Three different words are used, and the meanings are rather different.

In Song 5:6, the woman gets out of bed to meet her lover, who has come and demands to be admitted. When she gets to the door, she finds, as the verse says, "he had turned and gone" (*ḥamaq 'abar*). The basic meaning of the first verb, a rather rare one, is "to turn away," and she is disturbed and distressed that he was not there. In 6:1, at the end of the same long poem, after the woman has looked for her lover in the night streets of Jerusalem, she speaks to "Jerusalem's daughters," asking if they know where her lover is. They ask about him, and she replies with a *wasf* description of him, which like all such descriptions is vividly specific. And they then want to help her find him, saying "where did he turn?" Her reply is not at all specific. Their question about his "turning" uses the verb *panah*, which has the basic meaning "to face." We might almost translate the line as "in what direction was he going?" or "where was he facing?" instead of "where did he turn?" The verb asks for the direction.

In 6:5, the man is marveling at his lover's beauty, comparing her to Tirzah, which was apparently felt to be at that time a very beautiful city. He says to her, "Turn your eyes away from me / they are too much for me." The "turn" verb here is *hasebbu*, from the root *sbb*, which has the basic sense of circling, or going in a circle. The adverb *sabiyb* usually means "around." Here the turning has to do with turning her eyes completely away from him, because he finds them too troubling. It is possible that this verb has a connection with the last of the four, from 7:1, the motto of the famous poem that begins "Turn, turn, Shulammite / turn, turn so we can gaze at you." The essay deals with the question of the meaning of "Shulammite." Just what this turning signifies is hard to be sure. Clearly, it is a turning in order to make "gazing" easier. But might it be a turning in the process of the dances that the second mentions? I would simply assert that that is the meaning if I had not noted that Exum denies that *šwb* means that. I am not entirely convinced that she is right, though I must admit that she usually is.

CH. 7:11–14

אני לדודי ועלי תשוקתו
לכה דודי נצא השדה
נלינה בכפרים
נשכימה לכרמים נראה אם-פרחה הגפן
פתח הסמדר הנצו הרמונים
שם אתן את-דדי את-דדי לך
הדודאים נתנו-ריח ועל-פתחינו כל-מגדים
חדשים גם-ישנים דודי צפנתי לך

{she}

[11] I am my lover's, and his desire covers me.
[12] Come along, lover, let's go out in the countryside,
pass the night among the henna.
[13] Let's begin at the vineyards, see whether the vines blossomed,
the buds opened, the pomegranates[a] bloomed.

The Song of Songs

        There I'll give you my loving.

¹⁴ The mandrakes^b give   at our doors are all the fine
     out fragrance,   fruits,
   old as well as new;   I've stored them away for you,
             lover.

Notes on the Translation

a. "Pomegranates" appears in the next poem too. Linking word?

b. "Mandrakes" in Hebrew are *duwda'iym*, related to *dowd*, "lover," and to *dowday* (v. 13e, "my loving"), perhaps explaining why this fruit is sometimes called "love apples." Mandrakes (also known as mandragoras) have roots shaped somewhat like the two legs of the human form, which may have lent them a reputation as aphrodisiacs.

Commentary

In some ways this poem embodies the images of love in extremely outspoken and evident ways. Though the first line, "I am my lover's," might suggest that, it is less than the bald possessive it may seem. It takes the same form as in the book's title, "The song of the songs that are Solomon's" ("that are to Solomon"). Literally, "I am to my lover" can suggest something like possession, but there are stronger ways of saying that. Still, it means close connection more than anything else, and it is paired with "his desire," which is "over" or "upon" her, implying sexual activity. Love is surely present in the phrase, but we need to take seriously how the poem states it.

    Her invitation to a night in the rural field (I've turned "field" into "countryside") is followed by suggestive images of henna blossoms, vine blossoms, pomegranates, and mandrakes, which, except the last—if anything, the most sexually suggestive of all—have occurred before in contexts of love-making. There can be no doubt of the activities to which she is inviting him. I may have somewhat exaggerated with "pass the night," which translates *nalinah*, a term that refers especially to "lodging." Still, I see no reason to underplay the situation. Her invitation is unmistakable and delightful for all that. It is very interesting that this Israelite woman, speaking in the ancient times, proposes making love. So much for feminine passivity; nor is it the first instance of such a lead. However, though she is not always the aggressor, it puts a slightly different color on "I am my lover's." Such possession, in effect bestowed by the woman, is only one dimension of this multi-dimensional relationship, and it is one that has led me to perceive that the two major figures in the Song of Songs are very much equals.

The poem's symmetrical structure may suggest that very duality: two five-line segments of two + three lines and one four-line segment. These poems not infrequently have such symmetries, and even less variety than in this one. But the symmetry here is even more evident. It begins with *dowdiy* in v. 11a, the first line, and returns to it in its last line (v. 14c). The invitation to the *dowdiy* in v. 12a is matched by "my loving" (*dowday*) in v. 13e, and the whole is climaxed in v. 14a with the sound-play of "mandrakes" (*duwda'iym*). There is no hanging back from the mention of making love, and the mandrakes add their own emphasis in the form of a play on word sounds with an aphrodisiac vegetable. Like a number of the other poems in this collection, this one seems remarkably sophisticated, even if it is what we might call folk-poetry. We have here not merely repetition but also suggestive uses of related words. Such repetitions and connections may have made memorization somewhat more difficult for the person learning to be a reciter or singer, but the symmetry of form probably somewhat eased the problem.

CH. 8:1–4

מי יתנך כאח לי יונק שדי אמי
אמצאך בחוץ אשקך גם לא-יבזו לי
אנהגך אביאך אל-בית אמי תלמדני
אשקך מיין הרקח מעסיס רמני

שמאלו תחת ראשי וימינו תחבקני
השבעתי אתכם בנות ירושלם
מה-תעירו ומה-תעררו את-האהבה עד שתחפץ

{she}

¹ I wish you were my brother,   who suckled at my mother's breasts.

I'd meet you in the street, kiss you,   so no one could scorn me,

² I'd lead you, bring you   to my mother's house, who bore me,

give you wine, spiced   by the juice of my pomegranates.

³ His left hand is under my head,   his right caresses me.
⁴ I put you on oath,   Jerusalem's daughters,
how could you waken, how rouse   love until it wishes?

Commentary

The fantasy here is somewhat unusual. To wish her lover was her brother in order to avoid scorn on the street seems unusual, unless the culture looked down on public expressions of love by unrelated couples who are not somehow publicly promised to each other. Siblings who had been nourished by the same mother's milk might suggest that the common nourishment would introduce a likeness that would prevent social scandal: "Oh, they're just brother and sister." It is interesting that siblings might freely kiss in public. On the other hand, we may be talking about a village setting in which everyone knows everyone else. She wants to kiss him anywhere with impunity, though why anybody would "scorn" youngsters who kissed in the street is not clear to me. Perhaps some old fogies in Jerusalem's particular social makeup, or a village's, would do that, and some in today's streets might do it as well.

And why, if it were all right to kiss him in the street, would she take care to bring him for the spiced wine to her mother's house—notice: not her father's, which is somewhat unexpected. And to make the special point that her mother bore her, paralleling the breast-feeding in the line above, seems also almost too much information. Yet at her mother's house she wishes to make available very special wine, spiced from her pomegranates. Recalling that pomegranates have seemed a rather specific image of her sexuality (6:11; 7:13), and "mixed wine" was the contents of her vulva (7:3), the wine sounds very much as if it were a juice in something other than a wine-glass. Perhaps these codes are beginning to reveal some of their connotations.

At v. 3 the mode of reference changes. Vv. 1–2 have been addressed to the man, but at v. 3 it is "he" rather than "you" and "his hands" as the actors. Verse 4 is addressed to "Jerusalem's daughters," that chorus always interested in her descriptions of love-making. Here it is limited to a single couplet referring to waking up in some of the same words she used in 2:6–7. She puts the women on oath here against waking them, with two words clearly related, *ta'iyruw* and *ta'oreruw*, this time as a question rather than a statement, "how could you?" and omitting reference to the familiar gazelles and deer. And the "rousing" is not to be complete until *love* wishes. As to this waking: if they are not to be wakened, then is the whole poem, kissing in the street, wine in her mother's house, and his caressing her a dream? Not the first, I warrant. But all she says about that is "I wish you were my brother," in Hebrew *mi yittenka*, "would that you were" (v. 1a).

"Rouse" is the same word that appears in the next poem at v. 3c, and it may be a linking word like those we have seen earlier. Reference in the next one to the lover's mother differs from speaking in this poem of the woman's mother. But the two mothers may be another linking motif, using some of the same words.

CH. 8:5

מי זאת עלה מן-המדבר מתרפקת על-דודה
תחת התפוח עוררתיך שמה חבלתך אמך
שמה חבלה ילדתך

{daughters (?)}

⁵ Who is this[a] coming up from the desert,   leaning upon her lover?

{she}

Under the apple tree I roused[b] you;   there your mother[b] conceived you,

there she conceived who bore you.

Notes on the Translation

a. "This" is feminine, hence meaning the woman, as is made clear by "her," in the second line This line is identical to the first line of 3:6, but here we know that the feminine "this" is the woman of the couple.

b. "Roused" is the same verb as in v. 4c in the command to Jerusalem's daughters, and "you" is masculine singular, hence referring to her lover. I would see "roused" as a linking word there, as a reminder to a reciter about the next poem. Likewise the "mother" links from the prior poem.

Commentary

We cannot be sure of the speaker(s) of the first couplet. I suggest it might be "Jerusalem's daughters," because both the woman (feminine "this") and her "lover" are mentioned in the second line. That leaves the daughters as the most likely speakers. They were mentioned also in the prior poem, and we are used to their presence. The words of this poem are partly similar to words in that earlier one, especially "roused" and reference to the mother. To be sure, the mother in the other poem is her mother, whom she wishes briefly might have been his, and in this poem the mother is his mother. But any mother may readily serve as a linking word.

Again the location is the country, not the desert, which is farther out. And the couple is coming up from the desert. We must be reminded of 3:6, which uses the same line at its beginning. Here, however, unlike 3:6, we are told who "this" is immediately in the second line: it is the woman "leaning upon her lover." The tercet takes place where there are apple trees, hence likely a rural area, as we have seen it before. The contrast between desert and orchard is a very pronounced one, as orchards require some sort of irrigation. How close to Jerusalem at that time the line between desert and orchard came cannot now be determined. Most of the book seems to take place in or quite near Jerusalem, except when it is in the north near the Lebanese mountains.

The following theme of lovers making love where mothers conceived them is a contrast only in that the mothers are different, here his mother, and in the earlier poem, hers. It proposes an interesting continuity between the generations' lovemakings. In Jewish society at the time, continuity among the generations was evidently important, both to the elder and to the younger generations. In this poem and the earlier one, the continuities especially involve lovemaking in the places where the earlier generations did it. Here not only is lovemaking parallel between the younger and elder couples, but conception itself (or its legend) happened here to the older pair. No doubt the younger couple hopes for the same outcome.

Did mothers in Israel tell their daughters things like that? Did your mother tell you? Mine did not, but she was a Victorian lady, unlikely even to mention such things. And I see a picture of mothers in this book as very little like Victorian ladies.

CH. 8:6–7

שימני כחותם על-לבך כחותם על-זרועך
כי-עזה כמות אהבה קשה כשאול קנאה
רשפיה רשפי אש שלהבתיה
מים רבים לא יוכלו לכבות את-האהבה
ונהרות לא ישטפוה
אם-יתן איש את-כל-הון ביתו באהבה

{she}

⁶ Place me as a seal on your heart,   as a seal on your arm.
For love is as strong as death,[a]   jealousy stubborn as Sheol,
its flames[a] are fiery flames,   Yah's powerful blaze.
⁷ Floods of water cannot   extinguish love,
nor can currents[a] wash it away.
If a man traded   his family's wealth for love,
Everyone[b] would scorn him for it.

The Song of Songs

Notes on the Translation

a. All three of the words identified with this superscript have important double meanings. "Death" is *mot*, which means both "death" in its normal human meaning and the Canaanite deity in charge of death, one of the principal opponents of Ba'al, the Canaanite god of fertility. "Flames" is *Reshep*, here in a plural form, also the name of a god familiar from the Canaanite mythological texts, another foe of Ba'al, living under the earth and having a connection with pestilence. "Currents" is a plural form (*nᵉharowt*) ordinarily meaning freshwater rivers, sometimes ocean currents. In the latter meaning, there is still a third Canaanite god, Nahar, a sidekick of Yamm, "Sea," who was another major enemy of Ba'al as salt water, which is not friendly to plants and animals, and Yamm is sometimes given in the Canaanite mythic texts the secondary name "Prince Nahar." I will go more into these characters in the essay below, and also into Yah, sometimes taken as a reference to Yahweh, though many scholars think his presence here is only an intensifying suffix. I am intrigued by the presence of these names, in view of the frequent claim, which I myself have often made, that the Song of Songs is one of two books, along with Esther, in the Hebrew Bible that does not mention deities, including Yahweh. More below.

b. The referent of the plural subject of "scorned" is not quite certain. It might mean the "giving" and "wealth" as subjects of a plural verb, or alternatively "wealth" and "love." On the other hand, I suggest "everyone" as the verb's implied subject, hence the people who would do the scorning, and the particle *low* in the last line as "for it," namely the object of the scorn.

Commentary

Repetitions and alliterations are the major working elements of this poem. It begins with the repetition in the first couplet of "seal."

Then in v. 6c is the first of three repetitions of "love," *'ah^{a}bah*, in three different forms of the word: first uninflected, then in v. 7b with the definite article and the objective particle, *et-ha'ah^{a}bah*, and last in v. 7e with the definite article and the preposition "for," *ba'ah^{a}bah*. In v. 6d-f is a series of six alliterations on *š* (pronounced "sh"), including all four words in v. 6e-f, and v. 7c–d has two further repetitions of *š*.

The structure of the poem depends on sixes. Verse 6 is six lines in three couplets. Verse 7 is six lines in two tercets. That produces a rhythmic shift between the two halves of the poem, but the sixes show a balance between them.

Clearly the poem's subject is love. The central statement, "love is as strong as death," is followed by powerful images of fire in the last couplet of v. 6. At v. 7, we go to opposite images of water that nevertheless underscore the power of the fires. "Floods" and "currents" cannot "extinguish love" or "wash it away," implying its flaming qualities. Certainly the metaphor of the "seal" on heart and arm has centrally to do with love. It seems to be an image partly of hiding something (the cognate verb is used of sealing a letter, 1 Kgs 21:8, or a deed of sale, Jer 32:10) or shutting it away (shutting a house, Job 24:16). But it can also suggest the use of something like a signet ring to put a mark of possession on something. It is almost as if she is proposing to be the living sign of her possessing her lover, a sign that he installs on himself. And the seal is to be put on his heart, for the heart, as I have noted several times, was for the Hebrews the organ of thought and decision. So the seal on the heart pairs with the seal on the arm as signs of decision and of strength, strength supporting the determination that love is the quality of the couple's connection.

It seems unusual that these young people would think about love in terms of death. But "love is as strong as death" does not mean that it is stronger than death. Love cannot overcome death, but neither can it be overcome by death. And "strong," *'azzah*, does not propose powerful action, battle, for instance. As for death, it surely is strong, but it too does not suggest overt activity. We move immediately over to Sheol, the place under the earth where people went after death—not a desirable place, nothing remotely like the Christian sense of Heaven—not at all a "life after death." Sheol is if anything more passive than death, waiting for its victims to come to it, not going out in search of them.

Jealousy, on the other hand, is "hard," *qašah*, which I translated "stubborn." Jealousy, *qin'ah* in Hebrew, is mostly an opposite of love, but it also has a positive side to it, and can sometimes be rendered as "zeal." "Jealousy" and "zeal" are linguistically related in English, and "zeal" might even suggest a kind of powerful love. Does that imply that jealousy is capable of keeping Sheol at bay? Have we a convergence of these two very strong words for human feeling? Exum makes some important points about jealousy as being impossible to withstand.[1] If love's strength is equal to death's, then jealousy's or zeal's stubbornness is equal to Sheol's. Both sides of this comparison are, in effect, irresistible. She proposes that this is a central affirmation of the book, a proposition that I have no wish to deny. It is almost that "love" and "jealousy" are the irresistible alternatives to an irresistible realm of death. This thought surely comes closer to being a metaphysical move, than a psychological or moral one. One might almost suppose that the thought proposes the possibility of some kind of life after death. I don't think I would want to carry it that far, as I see no signs of such an idea anywhere else in the Hebrew Bible. To be sure, this book is so distinctively a singularity in the Hebrew Bible, that the thought of its having some singular ideas cannot be simply dismissed. I think I am not willing to go further than to say that love, jealousy, and death are importantly what reality is made of.

When we come to the flames that love suggests, we come to a fascinating problem. Love's flames are unique in this book. The one-word line of v. 6f poses a problem present only here. We have seen what seem references to two Canaanite deities, Mot and Reshep. But in v. 6f we may have a reference to the Israelite deity, Yahweh. The one Hebrew word in the line is *šalhebetyah*. The Ben-Asher text, now the standard vowelled Hebrew text of the Bible, records the word in that way, ending with the suffix "*yah*," the first syllable of Yahweh's

---

1. Exum, *Song of Songs*, 251–53.

name, and one of the forms in which it appears as part of personal names, such as Zechariah ($z^e karyah$, "Yahweh remembers"). Exum[2] proposes that that reading does not signify a flame belonging to Yahweh, but only an intensified form of the word meaning "flame," which she translates "an almighty flame."[3] That interpretation seems to me to give back what she wants to take away. She has read simultaneously both above and below the text. Thinking that "yah" does not signify Yahweh, but is an intensification of the phrase is reading below the text. Substituting "almighty" for "Yah" is, I think, reading above it, because "almighty," I believe, is not a philosophical idea that ancient Hebrews entertained. "Mighty," yes, but the extension of the idea to "almighty" is a philosophical move not present in my understanding of the Hebrew Bible. Many people think that Yahweh was almighty, and she intensifies the flame in that way. She points out, however, that the other major textual tradition, the Ben-Naphtali, reads two words, *šalhebet yah* [the text has a mark that doubles the last consonant], which could be taken as a reference to Yahweh. It seems as if we have the kind of choice where neither can be proven to be the right one. The delights of scholarship! I have decided to give "Yah" as the rendering, thinking that it is at the least a sidelong reference to Yahweh.

In this, I both agree and disagree with Prof. Martti Nissinen, whose article in the Exum Festschrift (see Clines, ed., Bibliography) covers this question. He concludes that "yah" does refer to Yahweh, but for reasons different from those that I find persuasive. Then by my lights he undercuts his argument, changing the Hebrew text by introducing a word not present in the text as it stands, and which he spells in exactly the same consonants as, but with different vowels from, those in the Masoretic Hebrew.[4] My objection to this all too common way of dealing with the Hebrew text is that, when you add a word to the text that the text does not have, you are rewriting the text, and I think that scholars have no right to do that with any ancient text. It's not that the text must not

---

2. Exum, *Song of Songs*, 253.
3. Ibid., 254.
4. Nissinen, "Is God Mentioned in the Song of Songs?" 279-81.

be changed because it is sacred, but that in dealing with an ancient text, we must not arrogantly decide that we know the language and usages of the ancient work better than the ancients did. I must point out, however, that I have committed a form of that very sin in taking a consonant out from the text of 3:10.

The reason for my decision about the mention of Yahweh is that we have in these few verses not one but four names of deities. In thinking that, I am shooting right across Exum's bows. She mentions all of the names in her interpretive essay but refuses them as names *in the poem*.[5] The others are the words I have translated: "death," "flames," and "currents." "Death" in Hebrew is *Mot*, the name of the deity in charge of death, well known in the Canaanite mythological texts found in Ras Shamra, Lebanon, as one of two principal opponents of Baal, the central Canaanite god of fertility. "Flame" is *Reshep*, a lesser but dangerous chthonic Canaanite god of pestilence and by extension of flame as the feeling brought on by fever. Evidently Reshep did not meet the approval of Baal. And "currents," *n^eharowt*, a word most familiarly freshwater rivers, is also in several places, such as Jonah 2:4 and Ps 93:3, ocean currents, which are salt water. The word is also found in that sense in the Canaanite mythological texts mentioned above as a deity associated with Yamm, "Ocean," who is the other main opponent of Baal besides Mot, and who is sometimes referred to in the texts as "Prince Nahar," Prince Current. Yahweh, of course, qualifies as the most important opponent of Baal in the Hebrew Bible. So this poem refers to several deities in Canaan, where Israel lived too, all of whom were opponents of Baal or associates of gods who were his opponents.

Does that mean that the names of deities in this poem should take precedence in our understanding over the more abstract, human, or merely geographical senses of the words? If we think of Mot, must we have in mind both death, as something all creatures experience, and Mot, the deity in charge of that realm? Must we think of Reshep as both an underworld deity of pestilence and, perhaps, fire, and the flames under his control? Must we entertain

---

5. Exum, *Song of Songs*, 257.

simultaneously the image of "rivers" and of "Prince Nahar," the deity present in, perhaps in some sense identical to, the Ocean and its salt water? And Yah(weh) has to do with the land, both in general and Israel's land in particular. I want to argue not that the deities should take pride of place, but that we must not ignore their presence in the poem. We in the Western world—and not only there—tend to make such a grand distinction between the world of human life and the world of deity that the thought that a given word simultaneously takes us to both is difficult for us. I think we must not only entertain that but embrace it. We deal constantly with words that are simultaneously on two levels: why not with these as well?

These four deities represent various spaces in the Hebrew concept of the world. Death has, of course, to do with the human (and animal) experience, and we enter it in the ordinary world. But it is connected with the realm of the dead, Sheol, which is under the earth. Likewise, Reshep is in Canaanite and Mesopotamian thought located in the underworld, but also, as involving pestilence, is present in the world. Nahar is basically part of the mysterious realm of Ocean or Sea, the watery world that the Israelites mostly avoided, unlike their neighbors the Phoenicians, who, speaking the same language, were great sailors and sea-going geniuses. But Nahar also has functions on the fertile land, as freshwater rivers, in which he is actually an ally of Baal's fertility. Yahweh, who in this poem and elsewhere, for example in the scenes at Mt. Sinai in Exodus, is flame, is mainly to be found in the Hebrew Bible in the land where Israel lives as its owner and overlord. Christianity moved him to Heaven, which in Hebrew is Sky, but the Hebrew Bible seldom did.

The poem is not finished with its difficulties. The last tercet contains some issues hard to disentangle. We should not be discouraged. We are reading an ancient poem that comes to us in an ancient language in a form that no one speaks any more. To be sure, people still read the old Hebrew in the Bible, but for the most part it is understood in terms that are current in our world. Those terms were not current in the world in which these poems came to be.

The final tercet proposes that wealth and love must not be commodities, to be traded for each other. Even in the modern world, we suppose that love cannot be bought—or if it can, the love is destroyed, turned into an object of public and general scorn.

CH. 8:8–10

אחות לנו קטנה ושדים אין לה
מה-נעשה לאחתנו ביום שידבר-בה
אם חומה היא נבנה עליה טירת כסף
ואם-דלת היא נצור עליה לוח ארז
אני חומה ושדי כמגדלות
אז הייתי בעיניו כמוצאת שלום

{daughters (?)}

[8] We have a little sister,	who has no breasts.
What will we do for our sister	the day she is spoken for?
[9] If she's a wall,	We'll build a silver battlement on her,
and if she's a door,	we'll circle her with cedar.

{she}

[10] I am a wall,	with breasts like fortresses,
Then I became in his eyes	as a bringer of peace.

Commentary

Who speaks the first two verses is unclear. They are plural, because they refer to themselves as "we" and to their relatives as "our." Because "we" in Hebrew does not distinguish gender, we cannot identify the speakers in that way, though most commentators assume that they must be either masculine or "Jerusalem's daughters." Exum determines on the single feminine speaker of v. 10, but she does not explain the plural pronouns in vv. 8–9.[1] I think that they might be the big sisters of the little sister, largely because at v. 10, we revert to a feminine "I," feminine because she boasts of large breasts, in distinction from the "little sister" of v. 8, who has not yet grown her breasts.

That proposes a problem whenever someone wishes to marry the little sister. The fact shows something about Israelite marriage customs: apparently girls could be engaged to be married (they didn't use that terminology for it) at what might seem to us a very early age, though specific information is lacking. The proposal of marriage, as in many cultures, was evidently the masculine prerogative, and the sisters are worried that a girl with small breasts might not attract the right kind of suitor. The suitor must "speak for" her, in effect lay claim to her. She is the passive receptor of the speaking. This structure seems rather different from and opposite to the equality of men and women we have noted elsewhere in the poems, the freedom of women to speak their minds and to act their intentions. The passivity required in this poem points in a very different direction, a structure that sometimes brought great heartache to young women, either because the men they wished would speak for them would not or could not, or those who did were too often simply unacceptable to the women for reasons of personality or age but were acceptable to their fathers. Bride prices were often significant amounts, and they went from grooms or grooms' fathers to brides' fathers.

Things become even more complex with what they intend to do for their little sister when someone makes the proposal. Walls

---

1. Exum, *Song of Songs*, 253–54.

and doors as codes are less than crystalline. Does the wall suggest a defensive device forbidding entrance, where the door is a means of entrance? The older women seem not to choose between the two, nor do they explain what constitutes being a wall or a door for a young girl. The wall receives decoration of an expensive and beautiful kind: a silver battlement. The Hebrew word is used in various places as a parapet or a turret or masonry courses. "Battlement" may seem somewhat excessively protective and military, and I would not wish to risk my entire reputation on the use of that word (though the NJPS translation and the NRSV did). I think of it as silver protection of the precious territory.

But if she is a door? That suggests entrance, and the decoration is more welcoming than defensive: a circle around the sister of cedar paneling, expensive and sweet-smelling wood, with a connotative nod to Lebanon, whose cedars were proverbial. But, of course, a door must be opened, and the word used (*delet*) tends to mean an open door, not a "doorway," often closed. Yet this door with its paneling "circles" the little sister. The image is ambiguous. Unquestionably she is being defended, but the sisters seem ready to listen to proposals to get through the barrier.

One of the big sisters speaks and contrasts herself. Although we cannot be sure whether the little sister is a wall or a door, we can be sure she has no breasts; the big sister is a wall and is possessed of large breasts, fortress-like, reminding us of the silver battlements in v. 9b. Is that clear as decoding? She seems to have her man already, and her fortress breasts are means not of defense or opposition but of "peace." The peace seems entirely between her and her husband and is contained within the wall. So "peace" takes place behind the defensive fortress that is her breasts. The man understands that she brings peace, which is her solution to the problem of walls and doors. The wall as fortress of peace is an unusual protective image for love, and it may well be an original interpretive decoding of her otherwise difficult code of the wall. But "peace" may alter the perception of both wall and door as actual or possible barriers to entrance. And she sees herself reflected in her lover's eyes as the one who *brings* peace.

CH. 8:11–14

כרם היה לשלמה בבעל המון
נתן את-הכרם לנטרים
איש יבא בפריו אלף כסף
כרמי שלי לפני האלף לך שלמה
ומאתים לנטרים את פריו
היושבת בגנים חברים מקשיבים לקולך
השמיעיני
ברח דודי ודמה-לך לצבי
או לעפר האילים על הרי בשמים

{he}

[11] Solomon had a vineyard   in Ba'al Hamon;[a]
             he gave it to the keepers.
    Each earned for his fruit   a thousand silver pieces.
[12] My very own vineyard[b] is right   the thousand pieces are yours,
             here,   Solomon,
    two hundred for the keepers for its fruit,
[13] You[c] who dwell in the gardens,   friends listen for your voice;

The Song of Songs

let me be the one to hear it!

{she}

¹⁴ Hurry, lover!   Be like a gazelle

or a young deer   on the spice[d] mountains.

Notes on the Translation

a. No place named Baal Hamon is known from the Hebrew Bible or any other source. From this, I conclude that the vineyard is fictional, here only to make a distinction between Solomon's (supposed) vineyard and the lover's own.

b. This expression occurs also in 1:6, where the woman describes being sent to tend the vineyards by her brothers, but she says, "My very own vineyard (*karmiy šelli*) I've not secured." Such a repetition very late in the book of a significant image from very early in it suggests a deliberate structure, though it does not persuade me to consider the entire book a compositional unity. "Vineyard" itself is a frequent image for the woman, and the repetition of the phrase from 1:6 suggests all the more that she is the subject of this line.

c. The "you" and "your" in v. 13 are feminine singular, and the "friends" are masculine plural. Therefore we are still in the man's voice addressing the woman.

d. "Spice" is balsam, and I have generalized it, as I think "balsam" is a metonymic allusion to the many spices mentioned in the poems.

Commentary

Solomon appears once more at the book's very end, in a way that underscores his position as a character, not as an "author." He is a vineyard owner, distant and wealthy, a counterpart to the local vineyard owner. Exum argues, rightly as I think, that this picture is fictional, especially as no place named Baal-Hamon is to be found elsewhere in the tradition.[1] So we cannot assume that this vineyard or its keepers and their incomes are genuine or accurate. "A thousand silver pieces" would seem a very high reward to one of multiple "keepers" for the vineyard's output. In Isa 7:23, a vineyard with a thousand vines is valued at a thousand silver shekels—but we cannot guess at the relation between the silver pieces and Isaiah's shekels, nor how the monetary value of silver changed between whatever were the time-periods of Isa 7:23 and of Song 8. This is love poetry, not economic history.

Whether the first tercet of v. 12 is a further fiction or not, and how it continues the image of v. 11—or does not—is less than certain. "My very own vineyard" must refer to the speaker's beloved woman, as the same expression, *karmiy šelliy*, appeared in the woman's voice in 1:6 as a definition of herself. Then perhaps the monetary references in the rest of the verse really refer to Solomon's fictional vineyard, and garble the figures somewhat. I think we need not hold the ancient poets to arithmetic subservience—their subservience to Solomon was quite enough. But the economics of the matter are strange. 1,000 silver pieces for the fruit belonging to Solomon, 200 for the workmen, is not excessively fair.

But at v. 13, the address changes to her. "You who dwell in the gardens" is feminine singular, as are "your voice" and "let me hear." That distinguishes him from his "companions," who are "listening" for her voice. We could take the preposition after "listening" as "to," but I prefer to think that the companions wish to hear what he requests to hear in the one-word last line of v. 13—he himself and only he. There is a difference between their "listening" (*qšb*) and his "hearing" (*šm'*).

She has the last word of the Song, and a familiar but sexy one it is. She wants him to "hurry" to her. The word sometimes means "flee," but here it seems only haste, not frightened flight.[2] The haste

---

1. Exum, *Song of Songs*, 260.

2. Carr, *The Erotic Word*, 137. Carr takes "flee" more literally than I wish to do.

is the kind that characterizes the animals we have seen so often throughout the book: the gazelles and the young deer, who have been companions before of both characters. The most suggestive image is "the spice mountains," which has so often referred to her sexuality. Mountains suggest the female body, as they have before, and "balsam" echoes 5:13, where she describes his cheeks as "beds of balsam," doubtless referring to delightful smells. We have seen many suggestive references to the fragrances of spices, and there seems no reason to doubt that she means the smells to suggest sexual attraction.

This book contains so much of splendid smells and other physical aspects of love, that we must suppose that the ancient Israelites—perhaps more specifically their poets, singers, listeners, and lovers—paid close attention to such experiences, no doubt eagerly sought them out. So love means, at least in part, the physicality of all the organs, sight, hearing, smell, and touch. In other parts, love it seems to mean appearance, often presented in metaphors of gazelles, deer, fawns, of mountains, colors, flowers, which also propose scent but are often visible as blossoms, as are the lovers' bodies. The sense that the natural world is full of delightful smells is a very telling proposal that we in modern times, depending so much on manufactured scents in perfumes and lotions, have lost touch with a world of natural smells that our ancient forebears knew and loved for their gifts to loving.

3

Assisting with the Translation: A Contemporary Poet Takes a Look at an Old Poem

An Afterword by Anita Sullivan

MY HUSBAND HAS TRANSLATED The Song of Songs from the ancient Hebrew. It's not as if this hasn't been done before. Why is he doing it? He's not sure exactly, but feels driven by an emotional attachment to the work. This could mean that his decades of immersion in the Hebrew Bible have laid down a set of instincts upon the contours of his inner geography—and these instincts, which are likely rare and formidable in their specialized capabilities, are telling him *something is still lacking, something is still there to be found . . .*

I respect that. He asked me to help him because I am a poet. I am also an editor for a small poetry publishing collective, a long-time amateur translator, and essayist.

But perhaps more importantly, I come cold into this work. I do not carry with me the usual Christian baggage of prior familiarity and reverence for the Hebrew Bible. I grew up Catholic, and never read the Old Testament, since Catholicism tends to emphasize the New. I never read The Song of Songs before this year, and

Afterword—Assisting with the Translation

I approach it with the critical eye of a poetry lover, hungry for beauty anywhere it is said to show up.

I remain an outsider in this enterprise. Yet reading various translations of this ancient set of love poems, as well as conversing with my husband about his work in progress, has overflowed into a set of questions and observations that may contribute something useful to the ongoing scholarship.

Preliminary Assumption: Poetry Is Formal Speech

One of my personal core assumptions about poetry is that it's innately formal. Not all contemporary poets would say that, but oddly enough, the general public would agree with me. The large segment of the public that does not habitually read or listen to poetry still believes wistfully in the existence of a separate, poetic speech, just as I do. The difference is that most people regard "it rhymes" as the only required formality to turn ordinary speech into a poem, and for the result to be a good poem it must not contain "fancy words"—i.e., too many adjectives, or terms you have to look up in the dictionary.

In approaching The Song of Songs as an ancient collection of love poems, therefore, I assume that its composer(s) and listeners were engaged in an age-old conspiracy to enter a special rhetorical space—a poetry space—whenever any part of this work was being performed. And bearing down with that assumption a bit more heavily, I assume that Song of Songs shares with all (or most) ancient oral-tradition poetry the convention that inside this rhetorical space prevails an entire secondary vocabulary apparatus special to the occasion. This is a distinct and stable convention, practiced and honed over thousands of years. What it condones is that "metaphor" is primary in poetic speech. That is, poetic code words do not substitute a second meaning for what we would say in "ordinary everyday" or "common" speech, but rather the poetic code is understood to mean what it says on its own terms. As if everybody knows everything in the world by two distinct but totally equal languages, and can switch them at will. As if Adam's naming of the creatures in the garden was a bit of silly joke, because someone else (maybe Eve?) was later authorized to name them again.

Love poetry is especially well suited to flourish within such a rhetorical space, because since the entire society is part of the conspiracy, all you have to do is call up the poetry trolley, and automatically you enter the safe house of the *other words*, where you're not violating the kinds of rules that might exist outside that space, that sanctuary.

In this sense, the obvious use of "code words" in The Song of Songs signifies a switch from everyday mode to poetic mode of speech, and it happens en masse as soon as the poem is brought into whatever public listening space wherein it was usually celebrated.

Second Assumption:
This is a Set of Poems from the Oral Tradition

I'm assuming that these poems formed themselves inside their culture by the usual crucible of human needs, whims, passions—and influences from surrounding cultures. I assume they were well-worn by centuries of speaking before this particular group was "called in" (so to speak) and written down. Very little scholarly work has been done about lyric oral poetry—the great body of oral tradition scholarship builds upon Lord and Parry's work, which dealt with narrative epic, and though there is some related scholarship regarding shorter works such as ballads (Roderick Beaton), grieving ceremony narratives (Steven Feld), poems and stories still active in the oral mode as nascent fragments of longer, more epic-like tales (Harold Scheub), I don't know of work that focuses on oral-tradition lyric poetry, and most especially love poems.

For my purposes in bringing a critical eye to The Song of Songs, I must assume it to be a somewhat random collection of individual pieces, preserved by a huge stroke of luck The poems strongly suggest to me the kind of repetition that would come from many different versions of the same little scene or situation. In other words, this collection swims into view as if it were a musical composition called a theme and variations. The poems work as a group depository of readily inter-changeable ardent, exuberant, young adult love statements. To view the work this way frees me from certain expectations I would have if I thought a single poet were responsible. I can stop asking myself, "Is this high quality poetry by the standards of its time—never mind the standards of today?" And instead I can listen to the poems in a variety of ways.

Always remembering we might not even understand the nature of the excellence of this work.

Always remembering that "theme and variations" can be a generative strategy, and for sure there is a feeling that something new and vital may have been struggling to crawl out from the "rhetorical space" in which these poems seem to have been festering.

Final Assumption: This Is Real Poetry

If poetry is to differ from prose, there has to be a reason. Much contemporary English-language poetry is really prose that uses line breaks to disguise it as poetry. Many poets are unable to summon the instincts that would allow them to reactivate ancient speech-generated proportional, tradition-sanctioned rhythms that signify the switch from an "ordinary" to "poetic" mode of speech. Poetic language is in the muscles and bones, it can't be imposed by a set of rules. We are a nation of people with ill-educated poetic bones—both for reading and composing poetry.

So how can we make an informed literary judgment about this ancient poem, especially when it's translated into English? In Hebrew, I am told by my husband and by other translators, the poem bristles with sound play, parallelisms, alliteration, enjambment, assonance, and other such prosodic devices—so that there is no doubt that these are at least *poems*, never mind their quality.

Informed instinct must be the final arbiter as to the quality of a work of art. I can only say, finally, that I do not know why this set of poems "gets through" to me, despite the many limits that the tradition seems to have imposed, particularly the repetitions of generalities such as "beautiful" "delicious," "sweet"; and also the

Afterword—Assisting with the Translation

somewhat wooden repetitions of code words such as deer, gazelles, goats, a variety of herbs, flowers and fruits, as well as a list of royal-treasury valuables such as ivory and silver.

Because of these vocabulary limitations, the poems can seem adolescent, naïve, as if they were the product of a rural and illiterate peasant class who may—like the folks Theocritus heard in third century BCE Sicily—have amused themselves by engaging in singing matches in which they mixed actual experience with romanticized notions of far-off worlds they had only heard about in stories.

The Codes

As with the so-called "formulas" of Homeric and other oral-epic poetry, what might seem to be the greatest weakness is actually the greatest strength. I'm making that assumption about codes and parallelisms in The Song of Songs.

Parallelism, as it shows up in English translations of ancient poetry, tends to bore modern readers because we see it as a sign of awkward redundancy. Translators often suppress or even outright ignore this device when they are trying to turn the old poetry into something exciting by contemporary terms. Parallelisms are sprinkled through The Song of Songs: sometimes within a single line ("my love, my friend," "like a gazelle, my lover, a young deer," "My dove, in the rock's clefts/in secret, in the cliff"); or in a two-line stanza ("a bundle of myrrh, my lover/ a henna cluster, my lover," "on his wedding day/the day of his heart's joy," "I was asleep/ but my heart stayed awake"); or it can take up an entire quatrain: ("I sought my life's love/ sought, but didn't find him/—"I scarcely passed them/ when I found my love."). Examples abound.

Here's why I think parallelism is more than a "mere device" (to quote James Thurber from The *Thirteen Clocks*). Because of the nature of language, no two words ever mean exactly the same thing. Therefore, laying down a synonym within a formal structure like poetry, causes a kind of nuclear fission, wherein an entire universe of possibility is laid open to the mind of the listener. Instead of clumsily reinforcing a single denotation, a parallelism hints

Afterword—Assisting with the Translation

at an infinity of directions out, and thus allows a simple truism to hold onto the full power of its original meaning, because the words—when reinforced by their close relatives—will not wear out. Thus you can get away with saying "I love you" and it will still pack some punch.

The same principle, I believe, holds true in the other chief poetic device that comes across in translation, which is the use of "codes" in The Song of Songs. Because these are love poems, and because they are highly unusual in that the male and female lovers speak to one another directly, and as equals, it might be expected that a code language would be needed to prevent the "grown-ups" on the outside from discovering what was really going on.

This seems unlikely for a number of reasons, but mostly because the code words do not function like equations, like similes, where it is relatively simple to nudge and wink and say, "Oh, yes, 'graze among the lilies' obviously means oral sex," and so forth. The possibilities for such one-on-one connections abound: nard, ivory, grapes, garden, vineyard, pomegranate, gazelle.

After puzzling over these code words for quite some time, I have come to respect them as a sign of high poetic skill—of a kind we no longer use in quite the same way. For the most part, the codes seem not to operate as similes or metaphors in quite the way we use them today. Rather, they act as "switching devices" to keep listeners constantly and vibrantly aware that they are inside an enclosed rhetorical space. Within this space, the code words fall to and flex themselves almost like small physical beings: almost like the language used in Old English riddles, where the solution to the riddle remains baffling because *it never was meant to be obvious*. Even for the original composers and listeners, there was always a gap, an ambiguity in the equation between the tenor and the vehicle—between the code word/phrase and its referent. This is actually the core of the creative vitality that remains evident in The Song of Songs. Language is felt to be crawling out from under words, as it always does.

Thus, even though The Song of Songs can seem, to a modern lover of poetry, to be tiresomely naïve in its use of sanctioned

Afterword — Assisting with the Translation

formalities, and tiresomely lacking in the daring poetic leaps from inner to outer realities that we relish today, nonetheless it qualifies as fine poetry because its limited language has carved out its own mode of operation within the rhetorical space allotted to it. Because The Song of Songs developed within an "assumption of poetry," then it found a way to behave as poetry. And, of course, as always happens when poetry is given an inch, it immediately takes a mile.

Bibliography

Alter, Robert. *The Art of Biblical Poetry*. New York: Basic Books, 1985.
Beaton, Roderick. *Folk Poetry of Modern Greece*. Cambridge: Cambridge University Press, 1980.
Black, Fiona C. "The Shulammite's Burning Bush: Passion, Im/Possibility and the Existence of God in Song 8.6 and Exodus 3." In *A Critical Engagement: Essays on the Hebrew Bible in Honour of J. Cheryl Exum*, edited by David J. A. Clines and Ellen van Wolde, 59–81. Sheffield: Sheffield Phoenix, 2011.
Bloch, Ariel, and Chana Bloch. *The Song of Songs: The World's First Great Love Poem*. 1995. Reprinted, New York: Modern Library, 2006.
Carr, David M. *The Erotic Word: Sexuality, Spirituality, and the Bible*. Oxford: Oxford University Press, 2003.
Clines, David J. A. "Reading the Song of Songs as a Classic." In *A Critical Engagement: Essays on the Hebrew Bible in Honour of J. Cheryl Exum*, edited by David J. A. Clines and Ellen van Wolde, 116–31. Sheffield: Sheffield Phoenix, 2011.
Dundes, Alan. *Holy Writ as Oral Lit: The Bible as Folklore*. Lanham, MD: Rowman & Littlefield, 1999.
Exum, J. Cheryl. *Song of Songs: A Commentary*. Old Testament Library. Louisville: Westminster John Knox Press, 2005.
Falk, Marcia. *Love Lyrics from the Bible: The Song of Songs: A New Translation and Interpretation*. San Francisco: HarperSanFrancisco, 1990.
Feld, Steven. *Sound and Sentiment: Birds, Weeping, Poetics, and Song in Kaluli Expression*. 2nd ed. Philadelphia: University of Pennsylvania Press, 1990.
Foley, John Miles. *How to Read an Oral Poem*. Urbana: University of Illinois Press, 2002
Fox, Michael V. *The Song of Songs and the Ancient Egyptian Love Songs*. Madison: University of Wisconsin Press, 1985.
Good, Edwin M. *Irony in the Old Testament*. Philadelphia: Westminster, 1965. 2nd. ed. Bible and Literature Series 3. Sheffield: Almond, 1982.

Bibliography

Griswold, Eliza. "Why Afghan Women Risk Death to Write Poetry." *The New York Times Magazine*, April 29, 2012, 38–57.

Kányádi, Sándor. *In Contemporary Tense*. Translated by Paul Sohar. Irodalmi Jelen könyvek. Island Heights, NJ: Iniquity, 2013.

Kugel, James L. *The Idea of Biblical Poetry: Parallelism and Its History*. New Haven: Yale University Press, 1981.

Landy, Francis. *Paradoxes of Paradise: Identity and Difference in the Song of Songs*. Bible and Literature Series 7. Sheffield: Almond, 1983.

Lénárt-Cheng, Helga. Review of Sándor Kányádi, *In Contemporary Sense*, Island Heights, NJ: Iniquity, 2013, in the Internet edition of *Rattle for the 21st Century*.

Lord, Albert Bates. *The Singer Resumes the Tale*. Edited by Mary Louise Lord. Ithaca, NY: Cornell University Press, 1995.

Miller, Robert D., II, SFO. *Oral Tradition in Ancient Israel*. Biblical Performance Criticism 4. Eugene, OR: Cascade Books, 2010.

Niditch, Susan. *Folklore and the Hebrew Bible*. Guides to Biblical Scholarship. 1993. Reprinted, Eugene, OR: Wipf & Stock, 2004.

———. *Oral World and Written Word: Ancient Israelite Literature*. Library of Ancient Israel. Louisville: Westminster John Knox, 1996.

Nissinen, Martti. "Is God Mentioned in the Song of Songs? Flame of Yahweh, Love, and Death in Song of Songs 8.6–7a." In *A Critical Engagement: Essays on the Hebrew Bible in Honour of J. Cheryl Exum*, edited by David J. A. Clines and Ellen van Wolde, 273–87. Sheffield: Sheffield Phoenix, 2011.

Preminger, Alex, ed. *Princeton Encyclopedia of Poetry and Poetics*. Princeton: Princeton University Press, 1974: "Allegory," pp. 12–15.

Scheub, Harold. *The Poem in the Story: Music, Poetry & Narrative*. Madison: University of Wisconsin Press, 2002.

Sells, Michael. *Stations of Desire: Love Elegies from Ibn 'Arabi and New Poems*: Jerusalem: Ibis, 2000.

Weitzman, Steven. *Solomon: The Lure of Wisdom*. New Haven: Yale University Press, 2011.

Index

addresses of speech, 41, 68
Afghanistan, 23
'ahabah (love), 43, 73, 131
Akiva, Rabbi, 7–8
'alamowt (girls/young women), 40, 106
allegory, 7, 8, 21, 24–25
alliteration, 37, 46, 130–31
almighty, 133
Alter, Robert, 9, 27, 53, 86, 116
The Art of Biblical Poetry, 15
Amana, Mt., 86
Amminadab/Ammiynadiyb, 109
Anti-Lebanon range, 86
antithetic parallelism, 15–16
'appiryown (palanquin), 77, 78, 79
apples/apricots (*tappuwḥiym*), 56, 58–59, 118
Ashkenazic Hebrew, 11, 12
Ashtar/Asherah, 87
audience, 59
awesome (*'ayumah/'eymah*), 106–7
'ayelowt hassadeh (does of the wild), 60, 64, 73, 74
'ayumah (awesome), 106–7
'azzah (strong), 131

Baal (Canaanite god), 130, 134
Baal Hamon, 141

balsam, 141, 143
banner, 58
battlement, 139
Beaton, Roderick, 146
beauty
   in ancient world, 115
   as awesome, 107
   blackness and, 46
   codes for, 54–55
   pomegranate as image of, 82
   as Tirzah, 106, 119
bed, outdoor, 55
bedaddero (because of what he said), 99
belly, 115
Beowulf, 13
Bible, *see* Hebrew Bible; King James Bible; *specific books of*
bidbaro (on his account, because of him), 99
blackness, 46
Bloch, Ariel and Chana
   Song of Songs, 9
bract sheathes, 99, 101–2
breasts, 83, 116, 117–18, 138, 139
breathing, 68, 84
bridegroom, 78, 79. *See also* king
brothers, 46

153

Index

camps, 114
canonical status, 7
Canterbury Tales (Chaucer), 12–13
caravan, 78
Carmel, 117
Carr, David, 74
   The Erotic Word, 21, 26
Catholicism, 144
cedar, 52, 55, 76–77, 79, 90, 98, 102, 117, 137, 139
chariots, Egyptian, 53–54
Chaucer
   Canterbury Tales, 12–13
Chermon, Mt., 85, 86
clefts, 65, 69
codes, 27–29, 42, 68–69, 146, 149
conception, 72, 128
construct relations, 37–38
couch, 53, 54
countryside, 49–50, 53, 65, 127
currents *(neharowt)*, 130, 131, 134

date clusters, 117
daughters, 55–56, 106. *See also* girls/young women (*'alamowt*); Jerusalem's daughters
David's tower, 82–83
dawiyd (David), 83
death (*mot*), 130, 131–32, 134, 135
deer, 27–28, 59–60, 64, 73–74
delet (door), 139
does, *see* deer
does of the wild (*'ayelowt hassadeh*), 60, 64, 73, 74
door (*delet*), 139
doves, 54–55, 102
dowd (loving), 43, 83, 121
dowday (my loving), 121, 122
dowdiym (lovings/lovers), 43, 93
dreams, 72, 99
duwda'im (mandrakes), 121, 122

Ecclesiastes (Qoheleth), 4, 7
Egyptian chariots, 53–54

El Shaddai, 60. *See also* Yahweh
En-Gedi, 54
Engnell, Ivan, 2
enjambement, 72–73
Erotic Word, The (Carr), 21, 26
errors, in copying, 10, 18, 76, 77, 109
essays, interpretive, 32
euphemisms, 100
Exum, J. Cheryl
   on *bidbaro* (on his account), 99
   on deities, 134
   on Egyptian chariots, 54
   on flame, 133
   on gazelles and deer, 60
   on girls as courtesans, 44
   on Heshbon, 116
   on house of wine, 58
   on jealousy, 132
   on *libbabtini* (captured by heart), 90
   on lionesses and leopards, 86
   on masculine verbal forms, 59
   on moment between waking and dreaming, 99
   on *nahar* (snorted), 46–47
   on palm spathes and sheathing bracts, 99
   on Solomon in Baal-Hamon, 142
   Song of Songs, 3, 18–19
   on speakers in 8:8-10, 138
   on "turn," 113, 119
   on vulva/navel, 113, 115
   on "What is this," 76
eyes, 54–55, 102, 116
'eymah (awesome), 106–7

Falk, Marcia, 99
   Love Lyrics from the Bible, 32
Feld, Steven, 146
female speaker, *see* woman speaker
fire, 131
flames *(reshep)*, 130, 132–33, 134

Index

floods, 131. *See also* currents *(neharowt)*
Foley, John Miles
   How to Read an Oral Poem, 16–17
fountain, 89. *See also* garden spring
foxes, 27–28, 67, 68
frankincense, 84, 86, 90

garden imagery, 93
garden spring, 89, 91
gazelle
   as code, 27–28
   commonality of, 116
   fawns as breasts, 83, 84
   grazing among lilies, 68, 84, 116
   man as, 64, 74
   oaths and, 59, 73–74
   similarity to "hosts," 60
gender relations, 8, 25–26, 68, 122, 138, 149
Genesis–Deuteronomy, 7
girls/young women *(alamowt)*, 40, 44, 106. *See also* daughters; Jerusalem's daughters
goats, 49–50
gods/goddesses
   Ashtar/Asherah, 87
   Canaanite, 130, 132, 134–35
   Ishtar, 86–87
   lack of in Song of Songs, 130
   of love, and gazelles and deer, 74
   Yahweh, 60, 132–33, 134–35
gold, 101
grapes, 118
grazing among the lilies, 29, 68, 84, 116

ha'ahabah (love), 73
hamaq'abar (to turn away), 118
Hamlet (Shakespeare), 14
hand *(yad)*, 100
hard/stubborn *(qašah)*, 132
hasebbu (circling), 119

head, 101–2, 117
heart *(lebab)*, 90
Hebrew Bible
   audience of, 29
   authorship of, 4, 6–7
   construct relations in, 37–38
   descriptive language in, 107
   modern scholarship of, 2
   parts of, 8
   poetry in, 13–14
   printing of, 10
   Solomon's authorship attributed in, 4
   as temple replacement, 8
   translations of, 10
Hebrew culture
   continuity between generations in, 127–28
   kissing in, 41–42
   as land dwelling, 135
   as male-centric, 26
   marriage in, 138
   as oral culture, 22–23
Hebrew language
   Ashkenazic, 11, 12
   Ben-Asher vocalization system, 11
   pronunciation of, 6, 11–12, 13, 14
   pronouns in, 27, 30, 41
   Sephardic, 11
   translating, 30–32
   verbal forms, 27, 30–31, 59
   "we" in, 138
   written, 10–11
Hebrew poetry, 14–15, 17, 18, 72–73
He kisses me with kisses *(yiššaqeni minnešiyquot)*, 41
henna, 52, 54, 89, 91, 120–21, 148
Heshbon, 116
hole, 100
holiness, 7
Homer
   Iliad and *Odyssey*, 5

Index

hosts, 60
house of wine, 58
How to Read an Oral Poem (Foley), 16–17

Ibn Arabi, 11, 74
Idea of Biblical Poetry, The (Kugel), 15
Iliad and *Odyssey* (Homer), 5
improvisation, 114
In Contemporary Tense (Kányádi), 5–6
incremental parallelism, 86
interpretive essays, 32
Isaiah, 7
Ishtar, 86–87
Israelites, *see* Hebrew culture

jealousy (*qin'ah*), 132
Jerome, St., 13
Jerusalem, 19–20, 106, 127
Jerusalem's daughters
    approach to, 19
    authorship of, 23–24
    dialogue with, 101–2
    encouragement by for love-making, 94
    oaths to, 59–60, 61, 72–73, 125
    at wedding, 78, 79
    Zion's daughters and, 77
    See also daughters; girls/young women (*alamowt*)
jewelry, 54, 83
Jews, *see* Hebrew culture

Kányádi, Sándor
    In Contemporary Tense, 5–6
karmiy šelliy (my vineyard that's mine), 47, 141, 142
king, 43–44, 54. *See also* bridegroom
King James Bible, 13, 40
kissing, 40, 41–42, 124
Kugel, James L.
    The Idea of Biblical Poetry, 15

Landy, Francis, 7, 20, 21, 86
lebab (heart), 90
Lebanon, 84, 86, 90, 117
leopards, 86–87
"let him kiss me," 40
libbabtini (taken my heart), 90
lilies, 29, 68, 84, 115–16
lily of the valley, 53, 55
linking words
    apples/apricots, 56, 59
    frankincense and Lebanon, 84, 86, 90
    function of, 2–3, 64, 91
    garden, 91
    gazelles, 59, 60
    libbabtiniy, 90
    mothers, 125, 127
    nadiyb, 109
    rouse, 125, 127
lionesses, 86–87
litter, *see* palanquin (*'appiryown*)
lock, 100
Longfellow, Henry Wadsworth, 14
Lord, Albert B., 146
    The Singer Resumes the Tale, 5
Lord of Hosts, 60
love
    buying, 136
    cross-cultural relevance of, 22, 32
    location of in body, 90
    as physicality of all organs, 143
    as strong as death, 131–32
love (*'ahabah*), 43, 73, 131
Love Lyrics from the Bible (Falk), 32
love-making
    as better than wine, 44
    desire for, 49–50
    encouragement for, 94
    food for, 58
    grazing among lilies and, 29
    invitation to by man, 65
    invitation to by woman, 61, 121–22
    preparations for by man, 93–94

Index

where mother's conceived, 127–28
  wine and, 43
love poetry, 9, 10, 17, 74, 146
loving *(dowd)*, 43, 83, 121
loving, my *(dowday)*, 121, 122
lovings/lovers *(dowdiym)*, 43, 93
Lowes, John Livingston
  "The Noblest Monument of English Prose," 13
Lowth, Robert, 15–16, 18
  On the Sacred Poetry of the Hebrews, 13

Mahanaim, 114
Maimonides, 11–12
male speaker
  as brother, 124
  descriptions of by woman, 54–55, 64–65, 101–2
  descriptions of woman by, 54–56, 82–84, 107, 114–18
  as gazelle, 64, 74
  identity of, 19, 20
  invitation to love-making by, 65
  as king, 43–44, 54
  love signifiers for, 90–91
  preparations of for love-making, 93–94
  as Solomon, 78, 79
  waking up woman, 99–100
mandrakes *(duwda'im)*, 121, 122
marriage, 33, 42, 138. *See also* wedding
men, 19, 46, 56, 68, 114
metaphor, 15, 116, 145. *See also* codes
meyšarim (right), 40, 44
mirror/symmetrical structure, 17–18, 41, 122
mixed wine, 115, 124
Moses, 7
"most beautiful of women," 49, 99
Mot (Canaanite god), 130, 132, 134–35

mothers, 125, 127, 128
mother's house, 72, 124
mountains, 143
Mt. Hermon, *see* Chermon, Mt.
"My lover answered and said to me," 63, 65
myrrh, 54, 75, 81, 84, 89, 91–93, 97, 98, 148

nadiyb, 109, 114–15
Nahar (Canaanite god), 130, 134–35
naḥar (snorted), 46–47
nalinah (lodging/pass the night), 122
nard, 54
našiym (women), 40, 49
navel, 113, 115
neharowt (currents), 130, 131, 134
nepeš (life force), 71
Niditch, Susan
  Oral World and Written Word, 22
Nissinen, Martti, 133
"Noblest Monument of English Prose, The" (Lowes), 13
non-parallel couplet, 60
nose, 83–84, 116–17, 118
nut orchard, 109

oaths, 59–60, 61, 72–73, 74, 125
Odes of Solomon, 4
Odyssey and *Iliad* (Homer), 5
oil, 42–43
On the Sacred Poetry of the Hebrews (Lowth), 13
orality
  improvisation in, 114
  linking words in, 2–3, 64, 91
  love poetry and, 17
  repetition in, 5, 105, 107, 122
  scholarship on, 2, 5, 22
  Song of Songs and, 1, 2–3, 4–5
  transmission process, 22, 103
oral-traditional lyric poetry, 5, 16–17, 145, 146

Oral World and Written Word
    (Niditch), 22
orchards, 109, 127

palanquin (*'appiryown*), 77, 78, 79
palm spathes, 99, 101–2
palm tree, 117
panah (to face), 118–19
parallelism, 15–16, 49, 86, 148–49
Passover, 33, 65
peace, 139
pendants, 54
penis, 100
perfumes, 54. See also smells, good
Phoenicians, 135
poetry
    in Bible, 13–14
    English, 14, 147
    Hebrew, 14–15, 17, 18, 72–73
    as innately formal, 145
    Kugel on, 15
    language of, 147
    love, 9, 10, 17, 74, 146
    pronunciation of, 12
    rhetorical space of, 145–46
    as something told, 6
    wasf form, 81, 101, 114
    "word" as rhetorical unit in,
        16–17
pomegranate, 82, 109, 124
Pope, Marvin H., 53
progressive parallelism, 86
Proverbs, 4, 7, 15–16
Psalms of Solomon, 4
pubic hair, 115–16
puns, 40, 44, 47, 83

qašah (hard/stubborn), 132
qin'ah (jealousy), 132
Qoheleth (Ecclesiastes), 4, 7
quwmiy lak (get you up), 63–64

ravines, 69. See also clefts
repetition

as art, 49
in oral poetry, 5
in parallelism, 86
in poetic structure, 130–31, 141
of related words, 122
as theme and variations, 146–47
transmission of poems and, 22,
    105
woodenness of, 147–48
Reshep (Canaanite god), 130, 132,
    134–35
rewriting text, 18, 133–34
rhetorical space, 145–46
riddles, Old English, 149
right (*meyšariym*), 40, 44
rose of Sharon, 53, 55
rounded bowl, 115
rouse, 60, 125, 127

sabiyb (around), 119
Scandinavian scholarship, 2
Scheub, Harold, 146
še'ahabah napšiy (lover), 71
seal, 131
ṣeba'owt (gazelle), 60. See also gazelle
šeḥarḥoret (blackened), 46
Sells, Michael, 74
Senir, Mt., 86
Sephardic Hebrew, 11
sexual morality, 8
sexual terms, 115
shadows, 68
Shakespeare, William
    Hamlet, 14
sheep, 49–50
Sheol, 131–32
shields, 83
Shulammite, 113
siblings, 124
Sicily, 148
silver, 52, 54, 76–77, 79, 137, 139–40,
    142, 148
similes, see codes; metaphor

Index

Singer Resumes the Tale, The (Lord), 5
sister, little, 138–39
šiyr (song/poem), 9, 38
slice, 82
smells, good, 54, 143
snorted *(naḥar)*, 46–47
Solomon, 3–4, 6–7, 9–10, 78, 79, 141–42
Solomon (Weitzman), 3–4
Song of Deborah, 14, 23
Song of Songs
   as allegory, 7, 8, 21, 24–25
   as anthology, 9, 19, 20, 38
   arrangement of, 27, 33
   author's change to, 77
   authorship of, 3, 6–7, 20, 21–22, 23–24
   completion of, 9, 14, 21
   composition of, 10, 22, 146
   conclusion on, 9
   errors in copying, 10, 18, 76, 77, 109
   as fiction, 10
   as fun, 118
   as Hebrew book, 12, 55, 135–36
   as naïve, 147–48, 149–50
   Passover and, 33, 65
   pronunciation of in Hebrew, 6, 11, 12–13
   as real poetry, 147, 150
   reasons for new translation, 1, 144
   scholarship on, 7–8, 9, 15, 18–23
   as single poem, 19, 20, 38
   speakers in, 19, 26–27, 33
   spirituality in, 26
   as theme and variations, 146–47
   See also Jerusalem's daughters; male speaker; orality; structure; woman speaker
Song of Songs (Bloch and Bloch), 9
Song of Songs (Exum), 3, 18–19
South Slavic oral poets, 5, 16–17

speakers, *see* Jerusalem's daughters; male speaker; "speaker unknown"; woman speaker
"speaker unknown," 19, 27, 78
spice mountain, 143
spices, 54. *See also* balsam; smells, good
spikenard, 54
spirituality, 26
"spread out," 58–59
spring, 65
strong (*'azzah*), 131
structure
   alliteration, 37, 46, 130–31
   enjambement, 72–73
   metaphor, 15, 116, 145
   mirror/symmetrical, 17–18, 41, 122
   mixing images, 82
   non-parallel couplet, 60
   opposite order, 49
   See also codes; linking words; parallelism; repetition
stubborn/hard (*qašah*), 132
Sullivan, Anita, 144–45
summer, 84
symmetrical/mirror structure, 17–18, 41, 122
synonymous parallelism, 15, 49
synthetic parallelism, 15, 16

tappuwḥiym (apples/apricots), 56, 58–59, 118
telling, of poetry, 6
tercets (triplets), 16, 17, 18
Theocritus, 148
thighs, 115
Tirzah, 106, 119
title, of Song of Songs, 3, 37–38
towers, 82–84, 116–17
"turning," 118–19

unknown speaker, 19, 27, 78

INDEX

verbal forms, 27, 30, 59
vineyard, 47, 67–68, 109, 141, 142
vulva, 113, 115

wall, 139
warriors, 78–79
wasf poetry form, 81, 101, 114
watchmen, 72, 100–101
water, 131. *See also* currents (*neharowt*)
wedding, 78–79. *See also* marriage
Weitzman, Steven
   Solomon, 3–4
wild, 73. *See also* does of the wild (*'ayelowt hassadeh*)
wine, 16–17, 39, 40–44, 57–58, 61, 64–65, 89–90, 92–94, 112, 114–15, 118, 123–24
Wisdom of Solomon, 4, 7
woman speaker
   authorship of, 23–24
   blackness of, 46
   as bride, 78
   compared to Tirzah, 106
   on delicious kisses, 42
   descriptions of by man, 54–56, 82–84, 107, 114–18
   descriptions of man by, 54–55, 64–65, 101–2
   desire of for love-making, 49–50
   desire of for lover to hasten, 142–43
   as faint with love, 58
   as garden, 102
   garden preparation by, 93
   identity of, 19, 20
   invitation by to love-making, 61, 121–22
   lionesses and leopards and, 86–87
   lover of as brother, 125
   oaths and, 59–60, 61, 72–73, 74, 125
   as one above all, 107
   searching for lover, 72, 100–101, 103
   as vineyard, 47, 67–68
women, 23, 40, 138
women, young/girls (*'alamowt*), 40, 44, 106. *See also* daughters; Jerusalem's daughters
word, as rhetorical unit, 16–17

yad (hand), 100
Yah, 130, 133
Yahweh, 60, 132–33, 134–35
Yamm (Canaanite god), 130, 134–35
Yiddish, 11
yiššaqeni minnešiyquot (He kisses me with kisses), 41

zeal, 132
zo't (this), 76

www.ingramcontent.com/pod-product-compliance
Lightning Source LLC
Chambersburg PA
CBHW030858170426
43193CB00009BA/656